The 7 Keys to Change:
A New Approach to Managing Change to Live Better and Work Smarter

William Matthies

The 7 Keys to Change:
A New Approach to Managing Change to Live Better and Work Smarter

ISBN: 978-0-9885262-0-4

The author welcomes your feedback. Email
wmatthies@coyoteinsight.com or call 714/726-2901.

Coyote Insight, LLC

the7keystochange.com
williammatthies.com
coyoteinsight.com

Printed in the United States of America

TABLE OF CONTENTS

PART I
Introduction: The Change in You

PART II
Getting Good at Change: Seven Keys to Get Where You Want to Be

ACKNOWLEDGMENTS

I must begin by thanking my clients whose planning assignments have been the foundation of Coyote Insight success for the last twelve years. Without you, there would have been no plan performance to reflect on, which, in turn, led to this four-year study and conclusions about change. You have my gratitude and—of greater importance—my commitment to do all I can to ensure that we both do better from this day forward.

I also wish to thank the over five hundred individuals who took the time to complete the Coyote Insight survey addressing change. You made an invaluable contribution. Your answers to my questions served as a benchmark regarding change for all who read this book. Those who struggle with change—as we all occasionally do—will now know, some for the first time, that they are not alone.

And from that group I wish to single out the contributions of those who agreed to talk with me, elaborating on their answers to the survey questions. Although it is important to know "what" and "how much," you provided the critically important "why." It was this "color" that brought to life what would have otherwise just been black-and-white numbers. Thank you.

And, of course, there are all the authors and consultants whose articles and books I read, some of which I have quoted in this book. Although you no doubt had many things in mind with your own studies, you couldn't have envisioned the affect your work would have on me. But that is the wonderful by-product of sharing ideas, each adding to the next, creating something new and positive in the process. Thank you. I have learned so much from all of you and now hope to help others as you have helped me.

I also wish to thank Caryl Wenzel who provided invaluable editing services on this project. Caryl's expertise, thoroughness, and patience with both my manuscript and me were all that I could have hoped for and more.

And, finally, thank you Paula L. Johnson—my website designer, editor, marketing consultant, conscience, and overall whip cracker—whose encouragement and suggestions, all balanced by carefully timed and deserved nagging, has brought this project to completion. Paula, you were right much more than you were wrong, probably much more than you realize. Thank you for your support, ideas, and hours of hard work!

Not Another One of "Those" Books

Thousands of books target business executives and promise to reveal the methodologies and science of change management. This isn't one of them.

This book was written for individuals such as you who want to see more positive results from personal and professional changes in life. That said, *The 7 Keys to Change* is a book managers should read to discover how to help themselves and their employees better manage change. Doing so is just good business.

Granted, some may not see the difference between existing change management literature and this book's purpose. Initially when I began this project, I didn't see the distinction myself. However, I do now and am indebted to many authors of change management and planning books, with some being cited in this book. Without their perspective and ideas, I could not have reached the conclusions and recommendations I'm sharing now.

But as with all topics, the goal of learning is to extend our knowledge and to build on the thoughts and ideas of others. So it is my intent that *The 7 Keys* will do that for you.

However, before going further, I confess that I didn't plan to focus on the process of change from the perspective of the individual; indeed, I didn't plan to write a book at all. Nonetheless, that is what happened (which I now believe for good reason), and I am convinced that those who read the results of my four years of investigation and then begin to apply the lessons I've learned will be much more successful in bringing positive changes to their personal and professional lives.

So if I didn't plan to write a book, how did *The 7 Keys* come to be? I'm a business-planning consultant. My job is to help management create plans that will hopefully produce profitable new growth. But what if what I do doesn't work?

In spring 2008, I began to think about that a lot. I always follow up with clients a few months after the planning assignment is complete to check in and see how things are going. This includes talking about the specific goals and objectives the plan was meant to achieve and asking management how much of the plan actually happened. Generally, although seemingly content with the results, the reality is that very few clients have accomplished anything close to 100 percent of the plan objectives or goals, with some clients achieving 50 percent or less.

To my surprise, no one seemed too upset by this. The clients cited many reasons that the results were not as expected, but "bad plan" or "bad consultant" was not among them. Everyone seemed pleased with what we had done months earlier. The lack of progress, they said, had to do with "changing market conditions," "general economic challenges," or "simply a lack of time to do what we need to do." But was it really as simple as that?

Some of my "consultant denial" (a protective shield that consultants naturally have, which helps us deflect responsibility to things and people other than ourselves) led me to conclude that most of this nonperformance was management's fault, not the conditions management suggested. I knew the plan was good, the client said the plan was good, and the client had paid me. However, if it wasn't me, the plan, or management's ability to execute the plan's provisions, what then? There had to be something more.

Consultant jokes abound, and many are based on telling our clients what to do while not taking our own advice. As with any good joke, there is some basis in truth. There are (far too) many practicing consultants who have never held a line job. They have never had to make the decisions they now advise their clients to make, and whether they know it or not, many simply cannot relate to the hard realities confronting their clients each and every day.

However, there is another group, of which I am a member, who in our past careers were on the "line" side of the desk. We know that with every important decision comes a potentially positive or negative result, and we don't take this lightly. So, because I have been in my clients' shoes, what should I be doing so that they might produce better results?

THE EPIPHANY

After thinking about it for some time, I realized I didn't know.

I had been successful as a line manager—both in my own company and in those owned by others. I am a successful consultant, with most of my business coming from companies I have worked for previously. However all that would matter little if my clients were not achieving the results we had planned for them.

Initially, I thought improving my consultation would amount to little more than reading a few books, gleaning the best information available, and simply adjusting my consulting methods accordingly. However, the investigation quickly expanded to include reading countless books and articles and talking with a long list of managers at private and public companies, from start-ups to large multinational companies, doing business around the world.

I reviewed my own history, looking for what had and had not worked, hunting for clues regarding the process that leads to success or failure. Although the initial focus was on business planning and change management, this quickly expanded to include nonbusiness self-improvement discussions, psychology, and sociology—literally any subject I could think of that might in some way hold the key to improving the chances for success. Finally, I went so far as to commission original primary research with a representative sample of over 500 individuals, no doubt including many people such as you, to understand their thoughts regarding change.

It soon became apparent that the concept was far more complicated than I had originally assumed. There would be no quick "one-size-fits-all" solution. I almost immediately saw that many of us in business had succumbed to false myths regarding planning and change and, as a result, had unknowingly erected barriers in our thinking that prevented us from achieving our goals. In my case, as a planning consultant, this not only limited my success but also spilled over to passively, negatively affect my clients.

I say passively because technically and in practice, my responsibility ends with the creation of the plan. The execution of the plan provisions is the responsibility of management; if management was not getting the results we all hoped for, that was on them, not me. However, this all began because I wanted to become a better consultant. As a result, there would be no technicality about it. If the client was not achieving the results it wanted, the results I wanted for the client, I wanted to know why.

THE REVELATION

Now, some four years later, my thinking has changed dramatically, and my consultation is the better for it. I clearly see the tight interaction between planning results and change management, for not only business but also all of us as individuals. And therein is the key.

Many look at the process for bringing about positive change in business as being completely separate from what individuals should do to manage personal change. Prior to beginning this project, I did as well. However, with due respect to those who feel this way, that just is not so, and the continuing belief to the contrary largely explains why so little business or personal change occurs as is hoped.

Whether you are a manager or an employee, my goal for this book is to help you see what is preventing you and your organization from achieving its objectives. However, of even greater importance, you will also learn what you must do to better address the personal challenges that affect all our lives. Make no mistake about it; the two are irrevocably linked. If you lack direction in your personal life, if you can't identify what you want to happen or what you want to become, there is little chance you will be able to help your business or company identify and achieve its goals.

Although this book frequently refers to business change, the critical lessons required to make positive change happen in business can and should, with little alteration, be successfully applied in our personal lives as well. Moreover, as you will soon see, successful change in business is simply not possible without the purposeful participation of employees who are at the same time individuals. Helping them proactively manage change in their professional lives is a requirement for business success in addition to helping them become more successful in their personal lives.

Although change is inevitable, positive change resulting from proactive effort is not. Like most people, you have often been subjected to change you did not consciously initiate with results you did not want, need, or expect. You may have attempted proactive change and not achieved the results you wanted. In that regard, you are like all of us. Whether we are reacting to change thrust on us, or initiating change ourselves, getting the results we want is never assured or easy. However, there is good news: There is a better way.

THE CHANGE IN YOU

If you or your company have never failed in attempts to bring about positive change, congratulations, both for having succeeded where so many others have failed and because you have no need to read further. However, the fact that you have read this far suggests otherwise.

For reasons you will soon understand, those companies that are largely successful managing change are few and far between. Indeed, large numbers of companies fail to even partially achieve their change goals much more often than they succeed, and, unfortunately, the results are no better and often worse in our personal lives.

Part I of this book sets the stage for all that follows. It begins with a statistical look at how we all view change, followed by a discussion of the nature of change, the results of efforts to create positive business and personal change, and, finally, the reason learning how to better manage change is the single most important thing any of us can do.

Part II describes the course of action (the seven keys) you can follow to create more positive change results in your professional and personal life.

PART I
Introduction:
The Change in You

Question 1
Which of the following describes how you feel?
(Percent saying statement describes them.)

62% ..... Change is inevitable; you couldn't stop it if you wanted to.

54% ..... I am generally very optimistic.

47% ..... When it comes to making change in my personal life, it's up to me.

46% ..... There is a lot I would like to change.

37% ..... I can change anything I set my mind on.

36% ..... Most of the change I've experienced in my life has been good.

31% ...... I get bored when things stay the same for too long.

31% ...... Change is neither good nor bad.

28% ..... Too many things changing all at once scare me.

27% ..... I get anxious when things change.

23% ..... I am content in my business/work AND personal lives.

19% ..... Changes in my job are very different than changes in my personal life.

18% ..... I love change.

15% ...... I am NOT very good at making change happen.

14% ...... I am content with my personal life but NOT my business/work life.

14% ...... I am generally very pessimistic.

9% .... Most of the change I've experienced in my life has been bad.

7% .... When it comes to making changes in my company, it's up to me.

5% .... If I had my way, nothing would change.

5% .... I am content with my business/work life but NOT my personal life.

CHAPTER 1

How We View Change

Before getting to the specifics of what change is and how to make the results of changes in our lives more positive, let's consider what a statistically valid sample of people (such as you and me) have to say on the subject.

The following summarizes the attitudes and opinions of 512 individuals between eighteen and seventy years old living in the United States.[1] When you look at their answers to questions about change, you'll see that your views are the views of many.

It is fairly rare in surveys to find things that "everyone" or "no one" "always" or "never" believes, but you wouldn't guess that based on how we talk—for example, "Everyone's going." "No one shops there." or "I am totally okay with that."

However, rather than absolutes, we find a wide divergence of opinion. And when it comes to how people feel about change, things are no different.

The first question sets the stage for all that follow, and there are only two instances where a majority agrees that the statement describes them. All others are below a majority (less than 51 percent); in several cases, they are low to the point of being—at best—a significant minority (approximately 25 percent) if not an outright small group (10 percent or less).

There is much to learn from these data and little way to define people based on just one answer. For example, the 62 percent who feel that change is inevitable include some of the 54 percent who say they are optimistic, along with the 14 percent who self-describe themselves as pessimistic.

The approximately 20 percent who say they love change is also a diverse group, including men and women of all ages, some of whom are content with the changes in their lives and some not. What about the 46 percent who say there's a lot they'd like to change relative to the 37 percent who feel they can change whatever they wish? Are they mostly mutually exclusive, with a few in one group also being in the other? Possibly but not likely. Identifying how you would like something to be is not the same as knowing how to make it so.

Perhaps the most important conclusion is the fact that there is so much divergence in these answers. This suggests that when it comes to change, there is conflict in the minds of many, and if that is how you feel, at least you know you are not alone.

OUR CHANGE "BATTING AVERAGE"

Each of us has, at many different times, in countless different circumstances, attempted to make change happen to our benefit. How has that worked for you? Are you happy with the outcome? Look at this group's responses to see how you compare.

Question 2 asked, "Have you attempted to make what you would consider 'big changes' in either your job/business or personal life?"

- Seventy-three percent indicated they had, whereas 27 percent indicated they hadn't.

Question 3 asked, "Was the change you attempted to make in your job/business, your personal life, or both?"

- Job/business: 15 percent
- Personal: 37 percent
- Both: 49 percent

Now for question 4: "How did your attempts at change turn out?"

- Very well, I successfully made the changes I wanted: 42 percent.

- Okay, but not completely what I had in mind: 35 percent.
- Not well; I was unable to make the changes I wanted: 23 percent.

Three of four people have attempted what they consider to be big changes in their lives, with half the changes being in both their professional and personal lives. And interesting for reasons you will come to understand later, only approximately 40 percent report complete satisfaction, with an additional one third finding things okay, and the remaining 25 percent indicating poor outcomes.

As an aside, imagine being a manager in a company charged with facilitating major changes in the way the company does business. If that were you, which of these individuals would you want to have working on your change initiatives? Who would you not want? Not sure? Keep reading.

THE CHANGING FUTURE

Question 5 asked, "Are you currently thinking about making what you consider to be major changes in your job or business and/or your personal life?"

- Job or business: 10 percent
- Personal life: 22 percent
- Both: 20 percent
- No: 49 percent

What do you think of the 49 percent who say they are not thinking about major changes? If you aren't comfortable with change, you might feel a bit envious and assume they have nothing to change.

This may be so, but possible alternative reasons for their answers include the following:

- They had just completed all the major changes they needed to make at the time they answered this question.
- It never occurred to them to think about change.
- People don't think about change until they are forced to.

Whatever the case, those not considering major changes will experience just as much change as those who are thinking about making changes. Change is inevitable, a fact acknowledged by two thirds of the sample. So what's on the minds of the 51 percent who are considering changes? Question 6 ("What changes are you considering?") provides the answer.

- Improve a relationship: 24 percent
- Where I live: 20 percent
- End a relationship: 15 percent
- Begin a relationship: 12 percent
- Career: 10 percent
- Improve health: 9 percent
- Have children: 7 percent
- Lose weight: 5 percent

The above categories in question 6 summarize detailed responses from those who plan change. These people are not only considering "career changes." They're going to quit jobs, find new jobs, seek or refuse promotions, ask for raises, transfer to new locales, work harder, slow down, and start or close their own companies.

This level of detail is also present for the other categories. They are investing time and energy considering what to do, whether or not the contemplated change is something they desire. Like it or not, ready or not, they understand change is on the horizon. But are they prepared for what that means?

CHANGE YES—BUT HOW?

At any given time, 50 percent of us are contemplating significant changes. You'd think we'd also have plans to increase the odds of success, but as question 7 indicates ("Do you have a specific way or process you use for changing things?"), far more don't than do.

- I don't have a way or process for changing things. I would just do whatever comes to mind: 61 percent.
- I do have a way or process for changing things and would use that: 39 percent.

Does a specific methodology help with the outcomes? Remember the 23 percent in question 4 who said they failed to make their desired changes? That number decreases to just 9 percent among those who say they have a specific methodology. Yes, a plan helps.

I'd even venture a guess that a significant number of the 9 percent who had a plan but failed to make their desired changes did so because they had the wrong plan.

Perhaps the most uncertainty comes when contemplating change in our personal versus professional lives. Is the approach the same for both? According to the sample, the answer is a resounding…we're not sure.

When asked if the process people should use to change something at work is the same or similar to the process they should use to change something in their personal lives, 36 percent said it was the same, whereas 32 percent thought the opposite. The remaining 32 percent were not sure.

You are correct if you assume there are many different ways to attempt personal and professional change, but remember the goal is not *attempting* change but *achieving* positive results. As you will see in later chapters, our collective track record in doing that is not all that good.

WHERE WE LOOK FOR HELP

Results aside, question 8 ("Which, if any, of the following sources of information have you used to better understand how you can make change happen?") tells us where people turn for help when contemplating change.

- Asked advice from friends or family: 53 percent.
- Read books about how to change things: 35 percent.
- Read magazine articles about how to make change happen: 28 percent.
- I haven't done any of these things: 27 percent.
- Talked with a professional, such as a medical doctor, a psychiatrist, or a psychologist: 25 percent.
- Asked business associates for advice: 14 percent.
- Attended a seminar led by someone who knows how to make change happen: 10 percent.
- Talked with a psychic: 3 percent.

The preceding suggests hope for authors writing about change, but still only one in three individuals rely on books. Slightly more than 50 percent are looking to others for guidance, many of which are equally at a loss. ("The blind leading the blind" comes to mind.) Lastly, the psychic community is at the bottom of the list, but "experts" don't fare much better. There is no clear agreement as to where one should go to learn how to make positive changes happen. Sadly, most people really don't know what to do.

THE ROLE OF BUSINESS

We've looked at how people view change, some of which will be altered by what their companies say and do. But how do employees feel about willingness of their employers to help them manage change—in the workplace and at home?

Although the musical refrain "we are family" may be as common in employee handbooks as it is at wedding receptions, when it comes to following through on such claims, the vote is split.

Question 9 asked, "As far as you know, when your company says it is 'family,' does that include the employee's family members or just the employees themselves?"

- It does include employee family members: 52 percent.
- It does not include employee family members; only employees are included: 36 percent.
- I don't know: 12 percent.

Question 10 asked, "Based on what employers do compared with what they say, which of the following best describes how believable a company's claim is regarding being a 'family'?"

- They include both employees and employee family members in the company "family," and the claim is believable: 50 percent.
- They do treat employees like members of the company "family" but do not include employee family members, so the claim is only half believable: 28 percent.
- They do not treat employees or their family members as "family," and the claim is not believable: 22 percent.

To a glass half-full person, the fact that 50 percent of the respondents said employers were family inclusive would be positive. The glass half-empty types would point out that 50 percent of the respondents think their employers fall into the dysfunctional family definition. Does it matter? It doesn't if employees have no personal problems, and, if they do, these problems do not affect their job performance.

Let's see what the employees have to say about this. Question 11 asked, "How often would you say your personal problems negatively affect your job performance?"

- Often to always: 17 percent
- Sometimes: 39 percent
- Rarely to never: 39 percent

It is possible that some people who believe their work performance is negatively affected by personal problems may be wrong. However, it is also likely that an even larger number of those who do not think their personal lives intrude on their performance may also be wrong.

Which do you feel is most likely? If you are a manager charged with making change happen through the efforts of either or both groups, are you willing to assume that the personal problems of employees will not be an issue?

In the end, you cannot help where help is not welcomed, so it made sense to ask whether employees would be open to offers of help (with their personal issues) coming from their employers.

Question 12 asked, "Whether or not your company offers to help employees solve personal problems, do you think it would be a good idea if it did?"

- Yes: 66 percent
- No: 34 percent

As stated previously, there are few absolutes in life and this is but one more example. The one third who say they are not looking to their companies for help will probably view attempts by their employers to help as an invasion of their privacy. But that still leaves two thirds who feel otherwise. The more a company can help its employees help themselves, the greater the probability that the company will also achieve its goals. This is good to know, but a more pressing question remains: "What now?"

With this snapshot of how individuals like us view change, we can move into discovering what change is all about, as well as the tools we need to bring about favorable changes in our personal and professional lives.

CHAPTER 2

Understanding the Nature of Change

"They must often change who would be constant in happiness or wisdom." —Confucius[2]

What do you think Confucius had in mind when he linked personal happiness with change?

Although advocating change, this quotation implies we have a choice, an option to simply hold things as they are. What do you think? If you could prevent additional change from occurring, would you? If you could have frozen time at some earlier point in your life, would you have done so? Would you do so now? Imagine what you would have missed and will miss if you could actually prevent change.

If we never crawled, we would likely never walk. If we never walked, we probably would never ride a bike and possibly never drive a car. Not engaging in sex all but guarantees we won't have children. No kids? Forget the grandkids.

Life offers numerous examples of conditional, sequential change resulting from a series of events, where each incident affects all that follows. For example, deciding not to study hard in high school may lead to grades that restrict the choice of colleges that we could attend, which, in turn, affects our career options.

Or agreeing to be part of a friend's wedding party might result in meeting someone who either becomes your soul mate or the other half of a very expensive future divorce. In either case, one thing clearly leads to another. And to this we can add nonsequential change—the events in our lives that occur in random order resulting in change that itself seems to come from nowhere. The outcome: We know things are different without always knowing why.

The underlying truth in each situation is that, for better or worse, something has changed; something ends and something else begins. Often, we had little or nothing to do with it or what we did try had little or no effect on what we hoped would happen. But that is the reality of change; some of it we initiate, much of it simply happens to us. Some of it we expect, whereas much of it comes totally out of the blue. Whether we initiate change or react when unexpected change is forced on us, the trick is to work toward the most positive outcome.

This is easier said than done; however, while making change work in your favor is difficult, it is not impossible.

I've never come across statistics telling me what percentage of change is self-initiated versus the "thrust on us" variety. Yet the fact that two thirds of adults see change as inevitable suggests that many might also believe that they do not initiate much of the change that occurs in their lives.

That seems right to me; however whether or not it is depends on the definition of what we try to change versus that we must change. Moreover, I've never seen evidence predicting how successful the average person will be in attempting to direct change to his or her benefit.

Managing change for our own benefit is the goal. The unappealing alternative is waiting passively for events to shape our lives.

This is all good and well, but who consciously thinks in these terms? Prior to this project, when I thought about personal change, it was like breathing or the weather. Change was just something that happened. Outside of business, I rarely considered how to attempt to improve the outcome of the many, seemingly inevitable events and shifts in my world. However, doing so is now a priority for me, and it should be for you as well.

BIG THINGS COME FROM SMALL STEPS

None of us will ever be able to favorably direct 100 percent of the change we encounter, but the goal is improvement, not perfection. For example, assume that 75 percent of the change that happens in your life is not initiated by you. How might that affect something as critical as how you make a living?

We are long past the era in which people can reasonably expect to spend their entire careers at one company. The world economy is extremely volatile and growing in complexity. There is little any one person or small groups of people can do alone to significantly affect what happens. Like a ship at sea, the most we can attempt to do is understand that ultimately we will encounter storms, and, as a result, we should do our best to prepare for what lies ahead.

However, the other 25 percent of this equation represents changes we can and should initiate. For example, be ready to find a new job, even when you're happy in your current position, by keeping your résumé and online profiles up-to-date. Start making plans to launch your own business if that's of interest. Proactively employ self-improvement career initiatives *before* you need to—before an expected change catches you by surprise.

Being proactive is not a cure-all, but taking the initiative in even a few areas of your life can greatly reduce negative outcomes (such as losing your job before you are prepared to find a new one) and increase positive results (such as leaving your job for a better position). Recognizing opportunities and managing change is a skill that can make an extraordinary difference, even if you start small. Is the time and effort worth it? Consider the cost of *not* doing so.

THE COST OF DOING NOTHING

The ever increasing cost of health care in the United States has been widely reported, but what might have happened had action to control costs been taken in years past? The Commonwealth Fund, a private group founded in 1918, whose mission is to address health care in the United States believes they know. They project that if the United States had implemented health-care reform during the Nixon administration, resulting in a 1.5 percent decline in the annual spending for health care, today's $2.6 trillion national health-care bill would be 40 percent less— a savings of over $1 trillion. Having done so even five years later during the Carter administration would have meant that our national health-care bill would now be 35 percent less. And if we had waited all the way to 1995 during Clinton's time, today's health-care cost would be just over $0.5 trillion less than it currently is.[3]

Is there a cost associated with taking the wrong action? Certainly. But these numbers suggest that the potential costs for not acting can be much greater.

THE BUSINESS TRACK RECORD

What about in business? Looking first at small business, we find what anyone who has ever started a company likely knows very well. According to the U.S. Small Business Association, 30 percent of all new businesses cease operation within their first two years of existence, with 50 percent doing so within five years, 70 percent within ten years, and a full 75 percent fifteen years after opening their doors.[4]

Clearly, the longer a company is in existence, the longer the list of reasons for going out of business becomes. On the positive side, the owners might decide to retire, decide that it's time to cash out, or want to live somewhere else. But the demise of a company can often be traced to a failure to react to competitive challenges, unforeseen changes in the customer base, or simple mismanagement. Whatever the scenario, the primary contributing factor is an inability to react to new realities. What is the bottom line? Management did not effectively initiate or react to change.

In 2002, McKinsey & Company studied forty organizations, including banks, hospitals, manufacturers, and utilities, all of which had been involved in mergers, major cost reductions, and/or new pricing strategy change initiatives. How did they do?

A full 58 percent failed to achieve their change goals, with 20 percent of this number achieving one third or less of their expected results.[5] Fifty-eight percent!

This was no fluke of the dot-com implosion that occurred in the then-recent past. A much larger 2008 study entitled "Making Change Work," conducted by IBM Global Business Services, found a disturbingly similar, dismal picture. In this case, the findings came from over 1,500 managers in fifteen countries representing twenty-one industries, with 14 percent of the companies employing over 100,000 employees and 22 percent with fewer than 1,000 employees. So, six years after the McKinsey study, how many were hitting their targets? The respondents indicated that only 41 percent of their projects could be rated as successful, with nearly 60 percent failing to meet their objectives.[6]

THE INDIVIDUAL TRACK RECORD

Over one half of business change initiatives fail, but how are we doing in our personal lives? Remember the survey data from chapter 1? Only 40 percent (almost exactly the same number from both the McKinsey and the IBM studies) of individuals reported satisfaction with their personal change efforts, with 25 percent saying that they had completely failed. When you consider that alongside the 50 percent divorce rate in the United States, at least when it comes to marriage, clearly we could be doing a much better job at handling personal changes.

When I first heard the divorce statistic some thirty years ago, I thought it was overstating the situation; however, even casual observation indicates that wasn't so. And new research tells us things actually get progressively worse the second (third, fourth, fifth, etc.) time around. Sixty percent of second marriages also end in divorce, with 70 percent of all third marriages failing.[7]

Tied to these figures is another indisputable fact: Failed marriages cost money—a lot of money. It's more than just alimony or child support; it is also the lost income that comes when two people no longer work together for the good of both. And, of course, this says nothing of the human toll exacted on one who must manage a single-parent household or the nonfinancial but very real price of growing up with only one parent.

The reason marriages fail is the subject of countless books, but each divorce represents another example of unachieved goals, which, although different from business goals, are every bit as real to married couples as they are to any CEO. Making even a small improvement, for example, a 10 percent to 15 percent reduction in the divorce rate, will have major positive impact that goes far beyond those directly involved.

However, change is not always about what *didn't* happen. As we've seen in business, at least 40 percent of people achieve their goals. But the question remains: How can we do even better?

In 1980, approximately 14 percent of high school students in the United States dropped out before graduating. By 1990, this number had decreased to approximately 12 percent; by 2000, it was less than 11 percent, and by 2008, the last year with available statistics, the dropout rate was down to 8 percent.[8]

This decrease in the dropout rate didn't just happen; much effort and resources were expended attempting to improve a negative and worsening situation. Was it worth it? Simple logic suggests it was, and we can only wonder where we'd be as a nation had we not turned this situation around. (And what if we had done even better?)

That these numbers would change was inevitable; that they will continue to change is even more so. However, the direction of the numbers is *not* inevitable, and, as a result, we have two options: (1) Do nothing and let come what may or (2) do all we can to bring about as positive an outcome as possible. In other words, we have a choice, and because we do, we can—to a degree—affect the outcome.

So what changed? What will change? Everything, literally, but let's consider a few items from a very long list.

- Every second of every minute of every hour of every day, 1.8 people in the world die, whereas during that same second, 4.2 people are born.[9]
- In 1970, the average U.S. hourly wage was $3.22. By 2009, this had increased 578 percent to $18.62.[10]
- From 1979 to 2009, the United States lost 39 percent of its manufacturing jobs, whereas professional and business service jobs increased 126 percent.[11]
- From 2008 to 2018, apparel manufacturing and related jobs in

the United States are forecast to decline at a faster rate (a decline of approximately 6 percent annually) than will be true of any other occupation.[12]

- During this same period, positions in management, scientific, and technical consulting services in the United States will increase at a faster rate (6.2 percent annually) than will be true for any other type of occupation.[13]
- In 1970, $1 had the same buying power as $5.63 in 2010.[14]
- The average height of the U.S. citizen has increased by just over an inch since 1960, whereas at the same time average weight has increased by more than twenty-five pounds.[15]
- In 1960, the median price of a home in the United States was approximately $58,000. By 2000, this had increased to approximately $120,000, rising in 2007 to slightly more than $260,000, the highest point. By 2010, the median price of a home had declined 35 percent to approximately $170,000.[16]
- In 2010, the U.S. household financial obligation ratio (the amount owed by each household relative to its income) was just over seventeen to one.[17]

Two people die every second, whereas at the same time four are born. Personal income has increased dramatically, with personal debt rising even faster, and prices going up as well. Employment is significantly different from thirty years ago, both in terms of the types of jobs and where the jobs are located. We are slightly taller, significantly heavier, and living longer. If you consider nothing more than these data, you could spend days thinking about the changes you should attempt to make to achieve your goals.

And due to technology, change now occurs at an accelerating pace. Consider the following quotation from a Wall Street Journal article discussing the rapid changes in business in an article ominously entitled "The End of Management":[18]

A popular video circulating the Internet captures the geometric nature of these trends, noting that it took radio 38 years and television 13 years to reach audiences of 50 million people, while it took the Internet only four years, the iPod three years and Facebook two years to do the same. It's no surprise that fewer than 100 of the companies in the S&P 500 stock index were around when that index started in 1957.

It should be easy to see yourself and many others you know in many of these numbers, understanding that all of this is not simply meaningless numeric change. The implications of these statistics (and many more like them) begin to explain why you are (or are not) where you want to be today. To make this clearer, continue thinking about the employment situation.

IT'S NOT YOUR FATHER'S JOB MARKET ANYMORE

How many of us now in the middle or second half of our careers really attempted to look ahead to what would likely happen when we were just entering the job market? I know I didn't. When I graduated from college, all I wanted was a job, and I gave little thought to how one industry would do relative to another throughout my working years. Things have turned out well enough but not because I ever gave due consideration to what the future might hold. In that sense (not having thought about it), I was part of the large majority.

Many, myself included, now believe we are going through an employment revolution, which, in terms of consequences, will dwarf what happened when the United States evolved from an agricultural economy to an industrial economy. This time, we overlay changes in the United States with worldwide economic reordering, with old jobs in one country becoming new jobs in others, and (hopefully) new jobs taking their places—jobs that many previously employable individuals are not trained to do.

My two adult sons both earned master's degrees in their respective fields, and I advised them to draft a strategy that includes their immediate goals as well as plans for their careers twenty to thirty years from now. As challenging as that is to do, it's as critically important to their long-term security as is earning their degrees and getting those first jobs. Consider why this is so.

Much of my early career was spent in the consumer electronics (CE) industry, initially as a senior vice president of marketing and product development for an American subsidiary of a large Japanese company, and later as the CEO of a market research and database marketing company whose clients were large, generally Asian-based, CE companies. A quick review of what has happened in that industry may help you understand how inevitable industry change can and does affect all of us.

My CE career began in 1978 when I joined Pioneer Electronics, at the time, an industry leader in car and home stereos in the United States. As was true for other then well-known brands, such as Sony, Panasonic, Kenwood, Alpine, JVC, and Toshiba, Pioneer's annual sales and profit growth were assumed as U.S. consumers eagerly purchased new car, home, and portable stereos in ever-increasing numbers.

Life was good; I loved my job and quickly advanced, as did many of my peers on both the manufacturing and retail sides. Some one-location mom-and-pop stores grew into regional retail chains, and at least two, Best Buy and Circuit City, went national, each with thousands of stores employing tens of thousands of people selling billions of dollars of CE products each year.

Many look back on that time beginning in the late 1960s as the start of the CE industry in the United States, but it wasn't. Prior to the arrival of the Japanese companies, U.S. consumers bought products from companies such as RCA, GE, Philco, Admiral, Westinghouse, Emerson, Curtis Mathis, and others. Their products were primarily radios, and beginning in the early 1950s, televisions from big companies with well-known, respected brands.

How these then-unknown Japanese brands managed to not only compete in the United States but also quickly redefine, expand, and then dominate America's CE industry is a subject for another discussion. Of greater importance is what that enormous change meant to those who worked at the American companies, as well as to those of us who began our careers in the newly arrived Japanese companies.

A NEW DAY

Beginning in the late 1960s, if you were an American engineer involved in designing and creating new products and working for an American CE company, you might be in trouble. Japan quickly "outengineered" the United States, contributing to the rise of Japanese CE companies at the expense of their American counterparts. On the other hand, if you had experience in marketing, sales, or operations, you could transfer your skills to the Japanese companies or, like me, begin your career at a Japanese company.

But what most of us failed to appreciate were the implications of working in a foreign-owned company whose headquarters, culture, and language were different from our own. And as true as that was for the Americans, so was it true for many senior Japanese mangers, both those in Japan as well as those stationed at the U.S. subsidiary headquarters.

Although there were many strengths associated with foreign ownership, there were also weaknesses, some of which led to the next stage in the CE evolution in the United States. Change of an order of magnitude that no one saw coming began to occur.

Imagine sitting in a meeting at Apple Computer in the mid-1990s. You work for an afterthought computer company whose market share is approximately 4 percent, with little or no reason to think that it will change for the better anytime soon.

Then someone starts talking about an idea concerning a new product category that Apple should create. Imagine two characters: crazy idea person (CIP) and most anyone else in that meeting (MAEITM). The dialog might have gone something like this:

CIP: So here it is. We introduce a line of what the industry calls "personal headphone stereos."

MAEITM: Are you talking about the Walkman?

CIP: I am, but let's never call it that again. Walkman belongs to Sony, and even if it didn't, it's too "old school" and attached to what is out there now. I'm talking about something completely new and different. Small, more compact, elegant; a complete new design with music stored on a miniature hard drive.

MAEITM: Well, we cannot call it Walkman all we want but that is what everyone else calls it, and none of this matters anyway because there is no way we'll ever be able to compete with

Sony. They are the undisputed king of that sort of thing, and most everything else in CE as well. Their corporate DNA is audio. We can barely manage to keep the lights on with computers; how will we ever launch a viable competitive challenge to Sony's Walkman when none of the more established, larger Japanese companies have been able to do so? What, based on better specs?

CIP: No, in fact our audio performance will be a little less than the best out there now because we will compress the audio file to conserve space. But that doesn't matter because we won't publish specs or even talk about them or anything else traditional audio companies talk about when marketing their products. We'll just talk about how cool our product is and show shadow figures wearing white earbud headphones, dancing down the street as they listen to music on our player—music they stored on Apple computers that they'll soon be buying more of from us.

MAEITM: Let me see if I understand you. We're going to introduce a new product into an existing market segment, one populated with many competitors but dominated by the world's leading CE company. And when we do, we'll just say our product is "cool", in part, because our specs aren't that good. Oh yeah, and this will also help us sell more computers when little or nothing else we've done has. Anything else we should know?

CIP: That sums it up pretty good, but because you ask, yes, there is more. We'll also open a music store on the Internet; one that sells music that initially can be played only on our products. We will sell individual songs as well as albums, all of which will have restrictions as to use. Initially, acceptance of this will be a bit slow, but I expect that within five to seven years, we should completely dominate the music industry, having changed the way music is bought and consumed.

Let's see…what else? Oh yeah, we'll also enter the cell phone business with our own proprietary phone and operating system, launching a battle by mobile carriers competing to be our exclusive partner. I estimate we should be able to sell approximately forty to fifty million phones worldwide during the first two years of existence, making our phone the most popular ever.

And, not to get too far ahead of myself, I see an entirely new type of…not sure what to call it; it's not a computer. Let's call it a "tablet" for now because it will kind of look like one.

It'll be cool and easy to use—just like our music player. I'm thinking we should be able to sell eight to ten million of them in the first couple of years.

And because of all this, I see our computer market share going up approximately 400 percent to 500 percent within the next ten to fifteen years.

With apologies to Apple for this fictitious dramatization, this is pretty much what it did and accomplished in the last ten to fifteen years. The Apple of today bears almost no resemblance to the Apple of the mid-1990s, but what has this meant to other companies, most of which were not in competition with Apple? And to those who worked at those companies?

SUDDEN, AMAZING, MAJOR CHANGES

For starters, look around your neighborhood and think about the stores that were there pre-iPod in the mid-1990s. Chances are you had at least one music store nearby where you could buy the latest CDs for $13 to $18 each.

You almost certainly rented or purchased movies from the local video store. You might also have lived near stores that sold only home stereo and video equipment in addition to a Best Buy or a Circuit City that did so, along with selling CDs, game consoles, game cartridges, televisions, VCRs, DVD players, cameras, and other assorted products generally referred to as "consumer electronics."

Although the equipment cosmetics changed over the years, as did the media (VHS tape before DVDs, vinyl records and 8-track tapes prior to cassettes, which, in turn, were superseded by CDs), the stores that sold all of that looked pretty much the same.

Then the iPod happened, along with the iTunes store, iPhone, and iPads. You only have to have been marginally conscious during this time to know what all that has meant.

The local music and video stores are all but gone, as are the stores that sold audio and video gear. True, you can still shop at Best Buy, but have you noticed the shrinking space allocated to CDs and DVDs and the lack of traffic in the audio and video equipment department? (When was the last time you shopped for stereo equipment?)

And Circuit City? They closed their last 567 stores in 2009 and laid off what was left of their 34,000 employees. In a relatively short period, the music and movie industries, as well as the companies that made the equipment that played songs and movies, have downsized dramatically if not outright disappeared. Gone too are the jobs and careers of hundreds of thousands of people, no doubt including some of you now reading this book.

Remember that I said my career began in the CE industry in 1978. I was fortunate to have fast tracked through several sales and marketing positions, ultimately becoming the head of marketing and product development for Pioneer Electronics for all their home and car audio and video products in the United States.

This wasn't a bad career trajectory, particularly for a thirty-three-year-old, but with that success came a hidden cost I did not see at the time. The higher you go in a specific industry, the more you become associated with only that industry. Potential employers in other industries view you as unsuited for their businesses.

Although good marketing, sales, brand management, and product management skills should be largely transferable to other industries, all too often employers outside the industry you work in do not see it that way, preferring to hire people they feel will "understand" their particular industries.

I spent just seven years at Pioneer before leaving to launch a market research and database marketing company that included CE retailers and manufacturers (Pioneer included), along with a growing list of non-CE clients. That worked out well for me in several ways, including one I never saw coming.

Years after I left Pioneer, the industry radically changed, along with the great majority of CE retailers and manufacturers. The result was consolidation, a sanitized term for widespread closures of what had been otherwise viable companies. With consolidation went the jobs and careers of thousands of individuals who had made their way to mid-level and senior management.

Even worse was the fact that many of these suddenly mid-career job hunters were stigmatized as "CE people," deemed unsuitable for employment in other industries. What had been good career paths were suddenly blocked, leaving otherwise well-educated and experienced managers looking for anything to support themselves and their families.

Researching this book put me in touch with many people, the great majority of whom were on typical career paths with predictable periods of unemployment and advancement through several companies. This was true of my CE friends as well, until the last ten years or so when, seemingly overnight, their options and opportunities evaporated.

All of a sudden, they were forty to fifty years old with fifteen to twenty-five years until retirement and twenty to thirty years invested in the CE industry, needing to look for jobs outside the CE industry. It has been very difficult for many of them.

I won't argue hiring managers' logic when they consider people with experience only in their particular industry; it just happens. However, even if you like what you do, you may not be able to make a career of it if, such as many in the CE industry, you one day wake up to see your industry no longer viable enough to take you to retirement.

Looking back, I'm certain that no one could have foreseen the order of magnitude of change that came to pass, all of which would have caused me significant career problems had I remained exclusively in CE. However, although you can't accurately predict where a particular industry will be twenty or thirty years from now, you can and should take steps to prepare for the inevitable change that affects many careers. In other words, you should attempt to proactively manage career changes, which, unfortunately, too few do in time—or at all.

YOU HAVE TO BE READY

My consulting business puts me in contact with a wide variety of CE and non-CE companies and management. As a result, I regularly hear from those looking for new jobs. However, unfortunately for them, I don't always hear from them when or how I should. As soon as a company announces it is "rightsizing" or closing, I see an immediate flurry of activity on LinkedIn, Plaxo, and other networking sites. Hastily added profiles appear with numerous requests to connect with me and countless others, soon followed by e-mails beginning with variations of "Bill, I've decided to pursue other opportunities…."

Although the changes that occurred have far exceeded what anyone predicted, they didn't happen overnight. No one in the CE industry, including me, saw this coming back in the late 1970s, the 1980s, or even the early 1990s. But by 2000 or 2001 at the latest, it was clear that the time had come to plan career transitions. Yet many continued on as though it were still 1985.

Although I've used the CE industry as an example, radical change is neither unique to this industry nor in any way over. Not only will things never return to what they were, but the rate of change will also accelerate. Put aside all of the averages and government statistics; you know the impact this has and will continue to have on you and millions of your fellow citizens. What will you do in reaction to all this change?

Let's make it easy. You have but three choices:

1. Do nothing and let come what may.
2. Attempt to bring about a positive result after the change has occurred.
3. Attempt to anticipate the change, plan accordingly, and be proactive—with little or no guarantee that your actions will have any positive effect.

What do you think is in your best interests to do? So, once again, what has changed, and what will change?

THE YARDSTICK APPROACH TO CHANGE

My first post-college job paid $9,000 a year, not much money when you think about it today. However, back then, the average price of a house in California was only approximately $30,000, so all things considered, not too bad.

Those of us in the early stages of our careers used our ages as salary yardsticks. "Make your age," the common logic went, "and you are doing well." This was hardly encouraging to a twenty-five-year-old then making $9,000 a year, but I knew things would quickly change, and they did.

A year later, I started my second job at $13,500 annually, followed two and a half years later by my third position (my ego had changed by then, causing me to now see them as positions rather than jobs) with a starting salary of $21,000, or only approximately $7,000 under my age-related goal. Six years into my career, one year after completing my MBA, my annual salary was $78,000, well more than double my age. But as luck would have it, by the time I got to this point, few of us still connected salary with age. Things had changed.

I now realize that although many of those career metrics were nonsensical, they had value. These yardsticks made us create goals and support them by simple plans to better ourselves. In the crudest sense, we were practicing some degree of change management, even though that term would not be in common use until much later. Without fully understanding the mechanics, we were attempting to control the changes in our lives. Our efforts were not perfect, but back then as today, most any effort was a good thing.

Notwithstanding the fact that I am now considerably older, I realize the need to be proactive, to attempt to shape the impact of the change I will most assuredly be subjected to. Often, change involves choice but so does attempting to avoid change. In fact, doing nothing may be the ultimate choice, although not the best.

From the mundane to the extraordinary, the simple to the complex, you name it, it is and will be different. Your hair's color, length, and style; the clothes you wear; your attitudes and beliefs; your friends, enemies, and relationships—all will be different in the future.

Almost certainly how you make a living, where you live, and the vehicle you drive will be different. Personal things, such as your diet, and, as a result, your weight, stamina, and health, will change. Your finances, politics, religion, strengths and weaknesses, and, in the end, your ability to function in this evolving world will change.

Literally everything about you has and will continue to change every single moment of your life. So once more the only question is, "What, if anything, will you do about it?"

This chapter opened with a quote by Confucius, one I believe is particularly apt in a book discussing change. Far be it from me to even suggest refinement to the thoughts of one history's great thinkers. However, were I to do so, it would be the following addition: "They must often *attempt to direct change,* who would be constant in happiness or wisdom."

CHAPTER 3

The Relationship Between Planning and Change

"Too much change is not a good thing. Ask the climate."
—Michael Scott, Dunder-Mifflin, Scranton Branch Office Manager (Retired), *The Office*[19]

Four years ago, when I realized that neither my clients nor myself knew how to bring about more positive change, my initial inclination was to simply brush up on my planning knowledge. I assumed I was missing something, so whatever it was, it must have to do with planning. There is nothing unusual about that; we all tend to gravitate toward what we know (although it is ironic because if we really do know "it," what more can there be to learn?).

So, I said, it's just a matter of reading some more current books on planning, discovering what I'd forgotten (or never knew), and get back to business. However, after browsing several current titles by well-known business authors, I began to doubt that this alone was the solution. I wasn't finding too much different from what I had learned so many years before, and certainly nothing that explained why so few companies achieved so few of their planning goals.

Once more, there must be something else.

My next thought was to investigate change management to better understand its relationship to planning (a plan envisions desirable change achieved with strategy and tactics that must be managed). The problem was not finding information on the topic but rather finding useful information.

At the start of my investigation, Amazon listed approximately 53,000 titles on business planning and some 12,000 titles on change, change management, and the like. Throw personal change into the mix, and that's an additional 110,000 books, many in the self-help section. Deciding which books to read was, to say the least, a daunting task.

Imagine all the books that have been written on any of these topics, in the shape of a pyramid, with the great majority at the base, not worth the money to buy or the time to read. As you move up the pyramid, you'll find decreasing numbers of books of increasing value and, at the top, a few extremely well-done. (And no, it is not lost on me that readers of this book will decide where on that same pyramid this fits.)

My search began by reading reviews about the books I was considering, which led to a long list of change management titles added to the great number of books I had already read on business planning.

Change management and business planning are similar in many ways and certainly related; however, they are not the same or interchangeable. Planning is how we determine what we wish to change (our goals) and what we will do to make things go as we wish (our strategy and tactics). In contrast, change management provides the discipline necessary to make the plan work (or at least improve the chance that it will work). Consider the following analogy to better understand this relationship.

Without effective change management, a well-constructed business or personal plan is similar to a vehicle driven by someone with no license, skills, or understanding of the rules of the road. Although such a driver could get the vehicle moving, the outcome will almost never be positive. And, of course, the reverse is also true. An experienced, licensed driver (business manager) isn't going anywhere worth getting to without a vehicle (business plan).

With books addressing planning and change management numbering in the tens of thousands, there appeared to be little for me to do beyond finding and reading the best available to become the more effective consultant I wished to be. Yet the more I read, the more I saw the disconnect between business planning and change management relative to the objective of goal achievement.

BACK TO BASICS

At this point, it may help to quickly review the major tenets of business planning, with the warning that this will be a gross oversimplification of what you need to know. If you really want to understand business planning, there is far more to it than what follows. And if you're reading this to learn how to bring about more positive change in your personal life, hang in there. You need this for reasons I will explain shortly.

The five major aspects of business planning are as follows:

1. Vision: The *there* we want to get to from the *here* we are currently at.
2. Goals: The specifics of what we wish to achieve. (This is sometimes referred to as objectives.)
3. Strategy: A general, nonspecific description of how we will attempt to achieve our goals.
4. Tactics: The specific tools we will use in keeping with our strategy that will hopefully result in us achieving our goals.
5. Review/revision: The continual review of our plan execution, including changes to tactics and possibly strategy, if we find the plan is not working as we hoped.

I have always felt this was a fairly straightforward description of what management needs do to successfully run a company. First, envision the big picture of what is to be accomplished (vision), followed by establishing specific, measurable targets (goals), which will signify success when they are achieved. To do this, management must devise an overriding approach governing what will be done (strategy), with the specific steps (tactics) that will be employed to achieve success, all with constant monitoring and change of the plan as new information becomes available (review/revision).

Simple—perhaps too simple? Yes and no.

It really is that simple, but, as always, the devil is in the details. Get any element wrong, which often happens, and although you will have a plan, it will be the wrong one, your chances for success greatly diminished. But could that alone be the answer? Could it be that nearly two thirds of companies were failing to achieve their objectives simply because their plans were wrong in one or more ways?

I seriously doubted that this alone was it. There had to be something more, and the deeper I got into the literature, the more I focused on the role that employees play in the process of plan execution.

A TEAM OF INDIVIDUALS

Most of the good planning literature makes clear that the rank-and-file employees will ultimately decide the fate of a company's plan. In addition, the majority of the better change management books say that after having set a vision for what is to be, management's primary responsibility is to ensure that the employees who will create and execute the plan's provisions are enthusiastic, knowledgeable, and capable of doing what needs to be done. Indeed, the books tell you, there is little or no chance of success without employee support and execution.

My thinking then turned toward the individual compared with processes and procedures relating to change management and business planning. If, as most of the better books said, the success or failure of change initiatives depends on individuals, it (to me) logically follows that the reason there was not more success must also have to do with individuals. And with that the case, I turned my attention to what and how the average individual or employee thinks about change.

The 100,000+ self-help titles on Amazon were written by authors from all walks of life, perspectives, and disciplines, including business, psychology, wellness, health, and religion. They ran the gamut from improving your life through yoga to how to grow rich by simply thinking positively. Although this was not where I assumed my answers would be found, I began looking for those titles I hoped would in some way affect the outcome of my research. And well that I did because there were some that had much to offer.

As an aside, had these self-help book authors known my intent, I doubt they would grasp the role their work would play in my initially business-focused quest, no more than business authors could imagine their advice helping individuals deal with personal issues. However, as will soon become apparent, had I not shifted my focus to the individual, I would not likely have found the answer.

Business planning literature tends to take a more structured, rigid approach using common business language: "We have established our corporate vision, set our corporate goals, and developed our corporate strategy, all of which leads us to specific measurable, effective tactics that, we are convinced, will lead us to successful results in the future."

That statement and others like it are the mantra of business books. In the self-help category, however, you'll find a more "civilian" language that initially bears little or no relationship to business planning. However, the more I read, the more convinced I became that they really are quite similar.

Although business talks about vision, goals, strategy, and tactics, in our personal lives, we talk about what we want to do, how we will do it, when we will get it done, at what cost, and who will do it. The "what" is roughly the equivalent of a business vision statement and the more specific goals that support that vision.

The "how" parallels the strategy and tactics portion of business planning. Any business planner worth the paper a business plan is written on will recognize the importance of defining when something will be done as well as how much it will cost.

Finally, no plan has ever executed itself. Whether we are talking about achieving business or personal goals, everyone should understand we have to identify who will actually do what needs to be done.

Notice the similarities. Define what you want, determine what you need to do to make it happen, and then get on with it. The differences are only in the terms used to describe each rather than how things are to be done.

Of course, few people approach their personal lives as they would their business or professional lives, with fewer still sitting down and writing a plan to govern their actions. Regardless of education, gender, or age, we tend to "wing it" rather than plan it, believing we know what we are doing.

So, is this a veiled suggestion that we should create a structured, formal plan to guide our personal lives? If we do, will everything—from our relationships with our children and significant others to our financial well-being, all the way to our summer vacations—be more successful? No. Most people (including me) never plan their lives to that degree. Still, understanding the basics and incorporating a "soft" approach to planning will produce better results.

We plan now, perhaps more in our business lives than in our personal lives—and perhaps not as well as we should in either—but we do plan. Yet the question remains: Why aren't we more successful? Is a lack of personal planning the reason we have so many personal issues, which, in turn, prevent us from being more effective in our jobs?

Yes but only to a point. There is still more to learn, and a good place to begin is by doing away with the separate "church and state" thinking we employ when it comes to how we handle change in our work versus our personal lives. They are different, but they also impact each other considerably. To see how, let's briefly consider one person's experiences.

PAUL: NOT WHAT HE APPEARED TO BE

"Paul" is in his late forties with a bachelor's degree in English and an MBA from UC Berkeley. For the last seventeen years or so, he's wound his way through several CE companies, starting as a product trainer for home audio products, ultimately working his way up to director of marketing for a nationally recognized television brand. I would like to say he has enjoyed what he does and that he honestly likes the products he has sold and marketed, but I am not at all certain that is the case. He has come off aloof and a bit angry as long as I've known him throughout our decade-long acquaintance.

Paul has never been one for small talk. I'd be invited to a meeting at the beginning of a project, and, along with other client employees, there would be Paul, checking e-mail, waiting for the meeting to start, talking with no one.

Whenever possible, I note the names of everyone in every meeting I attend, along with their positions and responsibilities. Sometimes this naturally occurs when we introduce ourselves and exchange business cards; in other situations, I get as much as I can from a quick verbal around-the-table introduction.

Before the emergence of social media, I'd file the business cards by company, keeping my written notes indefinitely. In recent years, although doing the same, I also check to see if the new people I meet are members of LinkedIn, Plaxo, or other business networks. Why do this? To be perfectly candid, you never know when a person will one day be in a position to help (or hurt) you. The more you know, the better.

I vividly recall the first time I met Paul earlier in his career, when he worked for a different company than he does today. Two other consultants and I were invited to sit in on a meeting to discuss potential large-scale changes the company was considering. Most everyone exchanged business cards before the meeting started—everyone except Paul.

Although he accepted cards from us outsiders, we had to walk them over to where he was sitting, and if he had his cards with him, he didn't offer them. The unspoken message was all too clear: "I don't want to be here, and you have nothing to say I want to hear." But he saved the best for last. When the meeting was over, he gathered his computer, papers, phone, and portfolio and then tossed our business cards in the trash as he walked out the door.

I concluded that Paul was just one of those individuals who prefers to live in his own world, interacting as little as possible with others. If so, he is not alone. Although his was an extreme case, at least in terms of his blatant disregard for accepted social norms, I have met many—perhaps even a slight majority of—people who just do not consider the long-term implications of their actions.

His coworkers seconded my observations about Paul. They agreed he was an equal opportunity offender, showing little more courtesy to his peers and subordinates than he did to people outside his company. He did manage to get promoted, but the general conclusion was that he did not up to his potential. He was obviously bright and well educated, but his complete lack of people skills restricted further advancement. This appeared to matter little to Paul—until his company downsized, eliminating his position.

"BILL, ABOUT THAT BUSINESS CARD"

Some time later, I received an e-mail from the same fellow who threw away my business card in my presence. Paul began cordially enough before zeroing in to ask for my help in making contact with companies who may be interested in his background. He also said he was very interested in my company and may consider joining me, believing he would be of great benefit helping me to grow my business.

This wasn't the first such message I'd received; I get plenty and have become pretty good at predicting who will ask for help. Not surprising, those who are naturally more outgoing or with whom I have a good business or personal relationship will reach out when it's time to find a new job. These folks get my support every time because I enjoy helping people I like, and I often get rewarded for having done so. If I help a client from company A land a new position at company B, I may end up with new business.

However, I also get requests from people like Paul who have never indicated that knowing me was of any value to them—until the day they need help.

Paul's e-mail was extraordinary in its audacity. He was not only spin doctoring the details of his departure despite widespread knowledge of his company's downsizing, but also boldly telling me how much he could grow my company. I was nearly dumbstruck by his seeming lack of connection between his years of aggressively off-putting behavior and his request for help. Had I acted the way he had, I could not imagine reaching out to someone I knew I had mistreated without first acknowledging and apologizing for my behavior.

Paul had no such qualms, and I can only imagine three reasons why he didn't: (1) He assumed I had never noticed his rude behavior; (2) he knew he was rude but didn't want to apologize to someone he didn't respect; or (3) he never thought about it at all. In any case, Paul focused on his primary goal of getting help with not so much as the word please anywhere in sight.

I am convinced that number three was most likely reason and certainly the most damaging to him personally. In the first and second scenarios, Paul would at least be cognizant of his actions. Change might be possible.

Paul's biggest professional problem was himself. He was simply oblivious; but the story does not end there. Although I told Paul to send me his résumé and I would think about companies that might be a good fit, my offer was not as benevolent as it may sound. I would never recommend anyone with what I considered to be unsolvable problems, and knowing Paul's personality, that ruled out many companies. I just wanted to see if there was anything I had missed that would change my thinking about him.

THE "OTHER" PAUL

Paul's résumé revealed a completely different person from the Paul I had known for more than ten years. Details about his education and work experience were familiar, but this Paul had spent years as a Boy Scout leader and a youth sports coach. How could someone so cold and impersonal at work be effective working with others, kids in particular?

Intrigued by this dichotomy, I asked him to tell me more about his volunteer work, and what happened next was stranger still. Cold, aloof Paul became animated, describing his passion for helping others and his desire to do even more than he already did. Thirty minutes later, I really liked this Paul and wanted to do what I could to help him. However, before I could recommend him to others, I had to figure out why his business persona was so different, as well as, if possible, determine to what extent he could change.

I told him I was very impressed with his volunteer work and congratulated him for doing more than most would ever consider. I said I would really think about where he might fit at the companies I worked with, but to do that there was one additional thing we needed to discuss. I asked him to tell me truthfully what he thought of me.

To my surprise, he did not sugarcoat anything. He said that although he had always recognized my intelligence, he resented the fact that (as he saw it) I could come and go as I wanted while (he assumed) making way more money than he. He told me there was nothing personal about it, and given different circumstances, we might be friends outside of work.

But the circumstances weren't different; our relationship was business, and that was how he felt.

As he spoke, I could see the old Paul returning with just a hint of doubt as he likely wondered if telling me this meant I would not try to help him. I asked how he felt about the other consultants we had both worked with, and he said more or less exactly the same. They had freedom and income he didn't, and although he knew that wasn't their fault, it bothered him nonetheless. With that done, I asked about his coworkers, and his response came down to them generally being nice enough to work with but not people who interested him outside of work.

Paul asked for my help, so I decided to come clean and tell him my reaction to both his professional and private personalities.

He listened attentively. When I was through telling him how much I liked the nonwork Paul, how at best I was neutral to the professional Paul, he smiled and said he was not surprised; he had heard this before. He didn't have any friends at work and didn't care because working was only a means to an end, a way to provide a living for his family.

However, he added, he didn't feel that was reason enough for him not to be promoted beyond the position he had just lost, and he was certain they had let him go because he was not part of the clique as he called it. He did his job and saw no need to go beyond that in terms of associating with others at work. Besides, he had let some of his co-workers know about his outside interests in hopes that they would get involved. But no one did and, as a result, henceforth his interests were only with his volunteer activities.

Because Paul so clearly saw the reality of his relationships with people at work, I asked him how he felt about those he came in contact with through volunteering. He had many personal relationships with individuals that went beyond their volunteer interaction. Their families went camping together, he golfed with a few of them, and they had dinners together as couples. In other words, these were real friendships clearly important to Paul.

Beyond simply volunteering, Paul was active in the management of some of his volunteer activities. He was president of his son's high school volleyball team booster club, which required interaction with other volunteers. However, when I asked him to describe his work relationships versus those outside of work, the differences became obvious. For whatever reason, Paul approached his volunteer activities with planning and forethought, allowing for differences in others, accepting compromise as necessary—and, of greater importance, he did so proactively. In contrast, he simply endured his job, not engaging unless forced to, and, as a result, he had little or nothing in the way of personal relationships to show for it. Moreover, in my opinion, his work persona was at least part of the reason he lost his job.

Often, we see people who act the same in most situations, but that was not the case with Paul. He demonstrated personality traits outside the office that would serve him well in his professional life, but he never let those positive qualities carry over. What are the odds that all the people he encountered through volunteering were worthy of his time and consideration, but none of his professional contacts merited the effort? Paul decided that his professional and private lives were completely unrelated, so he focused on one to the almost complete exclusion of the other.

LIKE IT OR NOT, IT'S ALL CONNECTED

Our business and personal lives are completely intertwined. Our personal traits affect our work lives and vice versa. We need to be effective at both, and the good news is that similar skills can be applied in both arenas.

Paul said he tried and failed to interest his coworkers in his nonwork life, but what he didn't say and may not know was whether what he did was too little too late. Whatever the case, the irony is clear: Had he treated his career like his volunteer work, the outcome could have very well been different. He would have benefited professionally, and his causes may have gained the support of his coworkers.

Keep this in mind as we consider the reasons that keep us from achieving more success—be it in our professional or personal lives.

CHAPTER 4

Why Positive Change Does Not Happen More Often

According to McKinsey and IBM research, as much as two thirds of business change initiatives fail. Two thirds! The specific industry, available resources, and the size of a company seemingly make little or no difference. Nor does management's approach, experience, length of tenure, and quality in directing operations. Neither does the emphasis on professional management techniques developed in the last fifty years.

With all that has been written regarding management by objectives, change management, and planning, the best we can do is hit 40 percent of *some* of our goals *some* of the time?

Once again, I concluded there *must* be something more, something not yet recognized that would be the key to understanding why so many otherwise accomplished management teams fail to reach their objectives. Certainly with tens of thousands of books written by so many business and academic professionals, the answer must be out there.

UP WITH PEOPLE

Most of what has been written is about processes and techniques, not people. Many books make it clear that success can come only from the employees responsible for executing a plan or the change initiative. But that's not the same as focusing on the people themselves. Few business books refer to employees as individuals, whereas self-help books and articles talk about people but rarely mention business or employees.

When it comes to planning and change initiatives, has business all but eliminated the human element from real consideration? And although recognizing the importance of people, have self-help authors missed the tie-in to business? If either is true (I believe both are), the effect on change initiative performance in our business and personal lives will be profound.

Management's focus is on changing things. No matter how much lip service is devoted to getting buy-in from those responsible for bringing about change, it's still more about process than people. Thus the only surprising thing about a 60 percent failure rate is that it's not higher.

THE PROBLEM WITH MANAGEMENT

I'm not alone in questioning management's orientation toward change initiatives; others have reached similar conclusions. In her book *Don't Bring It to Work: Breaking the Family Patterns That Limit Success*, Sylvia LaFair, PhD, says the following about management's tendency to analyze pieces rather than the whole: "…business is still largely shaped by analytic thinking, an intellectual orientation marked by a tendency to understand living things not by looking at the organic wholes that they are, but by separating them into their component parts."[20]

She's right. Significant change is not likely without considering the whole versus any singular part, which most definitely includes the people charged with making change happen. Certainly management must concern itself with plant, equipment, finances, and the like, but without people, the rest means very little.

As obvious as this should be, why isn't there a more clear indication of the problem to others? The *Wall Street Journal* may have the answer in "The End of Management" article: "The best corporate managers have become, in a sense, enemies of the Corporation. The reasons for this are clear enough. Corporations are bureaucracies and managers are bureaucrats. Their fundamental tendency is toward self-perpetuation. They are, almost by definition, resistant to change."[21]

Delete the word "almost," and I agree wholeheartedly. But while the article tells us what management has become, it does not explain *why* managers are the way they are. Without knowing that, corrective action is very difficult.

If the best corporate managers are resistant to change, the key is to understand why so that we can attempt to change their behavior before attempting to change anything else.

FIVE OBSTACLES TO BUSINESS CHANGE

By combining what others have said with what I am convinced is the "missing link" (a lack of attention paid to personal issues), I identify five reasons (or obstacles) why positive business change does not happen more often:

1. Management does not understand the planning or change management process it must follow to achieve results.
2. Management sets the wrong goals, often confusing goals with tactics.
3. Employees, who will be expected to do most of what is required, do not understand the planning or change management process.
4. Unresolved employee personal problems make it extremely difficult—if not impossible—for workers to be effective, in not only their regular jobs but also doing their part in the company change initiatives.
5. A combination of one or more of the above.

Let's consider each of these individually, with particular emphasis on the fourth reason.

THEY JUST DON'T GET IT

Management does not understand the planning or change management process it must follow to achieve results.

Management teams are indoctrinated with management methods and techniques. How could any management not possess some if not complete appreciation of the tenets of planning and change management?

Philip Kotler, S.C. Johnson & Son Distinguished Professor of International Marketing at Northwestern University's Kellogg School of Management and a celebrated business author, said, "All firms carry out some planning. However, while all firms plan, they vary considerably in how extensively, thoroughly, and formally they do it. Some managements are so embroiled in daily operations that they give little time to long-range thinking, let alone planning."[22]

This is true of a lot of management. Understanding that planning includes such things as vision and mission statements, the establishment of goals and objectives, the development of strategies and tactics, and other related planning jargon still does not guarantee the successful creation or the effective execution of a good plan. Moreover, good planning unaccompanied by a clear understanding of the importance of change management, including how it differs from planning, will almost certainly diminish the value of the plan to the point of uselessness.

In looking back at the various management teams I have encountered in my work, I realized that there were far more differences than similarities in their approaches to planning and execution. If this really was a science, or at least something that could be related to specific techniques, why do these differences exist?

The different approaches to planning exist not because management consciously alters the rules of planning and change management but because they do so unknowingly. As Kotler pointed out, added to this is the extra burden of having too little time to plan, the result of being so busy doing their day-to-day jobs, which is even more true now given all the staff reductions of the past few years. However, regardless of the reason, the result is the same: performance below that which is desired and expected.

OR THEY ARE CONFUSED

Management sets the wrong goals, often confusing goals with tactics.

To say management is generally aware of the basic elements of planning is not to conclude that they fully understand the relationship of one element to the next. One of the most confusing aspects of planning is goal identification.

Consider a company that is committed to a goal of cost reduction. If management then authorizes a 20 percent increase in staff, the staff-related costs will rise accordingly. Obvious—right?

However, goal identification is not as clear-cut as this example suggests. Companies commit to incorrect (and often unattainable) goals because goals and tactics are sometimes confused.

Business plans often include goals such as increase sales, achieve sales of $X, or other sales-related descriptors. Whether sales targets should be used as a goal depends largely on other factors, such as the objectives of the owners. For example, increased sales may not be desirable if a business is to be sold soon, presuming that the cost of increasing sales will reduce profit in the short term.

Of greatest importance, therefore, is that the goals must reflect the overriding purpose of an organization. Increasing sales may well be part of the company's agenda, but, in many cases, increasing sales might be a better tactic—one that will lead to the achievement of some higher order goal.

BUT DO EMPLOYEES KNOW WHAT TO DO?

Employees, who will be expected to do most of what is required, do not understand the planning or change management process.

The first two reasons business change does not happen are specifically related to management. But the success or failure of every plan, and, by extension, all significant change initiatives, is determined by the ability of employees who must do the work.

Good planning literature makes it clear that success depends on the involvement of employees—not only management—and this is absolutely true in change management. No matter how accomplished management might be, no matter how thorough its understanding of planning and change management techniques, without effective participation by the key employees, and ultimately the majority of all employees, the chances of goal achievement will be greatly diminished.

The key is getting employee buy-in to not only achieve goals but also support the methods for achieving the goals. Why is this so problematic? It's the knowledge gap. Although management may have been exposed to planning and change management techniques, the same is not true for many others in a company. What are the chances that large numbers of employees, many of whom do not have a formal business education, will know what they need to know to effectively participate in the change process?

The critical first step is to determine what employees do and do not know about planning and change management, making certain the key concepts are understood. This is rarely done; as a result, the very individuals who will be charged with creating and executing the plan know almost nothing about how to do it.

BUT EVEN WHEN THEY DO KNOW…

Unresolved employee personal problems make it extremely difficult—if not impossible—for workers to be effective, in not only their regular jobs but also doing their part in the company change initiatives.

If an employee is preoccupied with personal challenges, how effective will he or she be in helping a company achieve its goals? In a perfect world, employees leave personal problems at home and focus on a company's problems, planning, and goals during company time—in a perfect world!

As this book goes to press, the United States, and the world in general, is slowly emerging from what has been the most traumatic economic upheaval since the Great Depression. For many, this was the result of bad economic policy; for others, it was a normal, albeit severe, cyclical economic downturn. Regardless of the cause, the implication of a prolonged recession is far more than that.

There is significant and growing evidence to suggest that the world's economic systems are going through a major reboot similar to the period when economies evolved from being agricultural to industrial based, and later from being manufacturing to technology based. With that came not only a short-term correction but also a system that is largely different from its predecessor.

Much conventional wisdom about the economy is no longer valid. The tenets on which many of us have planned our economic lives (e.g., real estate value appreciation, easy credit, and guaranteed employment), no longer exist. In short, we are on the doorstep of a new economic world.

This did not happen slowly; many of these former truths were turned inside out in a matter of months. Now hundreds of thousands—if not millions—of people can no longer assume they will have the economic future they envisioned for themselves and their families when they began their careers.

This goes far beyond realizing that the vacation home, boat, travel, or other perks of retirement are no longer a given. The rebooted economy is making many people focus on the basics: paying for housing and food, getting health care, and educating their children. A society-wide change in fortunes creates stress and pressure that can lead to the end of long-term marriages and relationships, increased substance abuse, and assorted other problems. As a result, few, if any, employees are able to leave their significant personal issues at home when they arrive for work each day.

Management may not have the desire or the ability to address the changed psyche of their workers, but such changes negatively impact the achievement of company planning goals, as well the successful conclusion of major change initiatives.

THE PERFECT STORM

A combination of one or more of the above.

The fifth scenario is two or three of the first four obstacles to business change occurring together—or a "perfect storm" of all four at once.

One of the most common combinations is the first and fourth obstacles. Managers who believe they know how to plan or manage change but in reality do not are far more dangerous than managers who understand their limitations. Add to the mix workers who are so preoccupied with personal problems that they are hampered or even incapable of effective participation in company change initiatives, and the chances for success are greatly diminished.

"BUT THAT'S BUSINESS, WHAT ABOUT ME?"

Because all this comes down to the need for performance by individuals, how much of this applies to you who must deal with personal problems? With minor semantic differences, all of it. Whether the goal is to improve performance in a company or deal with a deteriorating relationship at home, the requirements are largely the same.

In business, you need to understand the specific processes necessary to bring about positive change, which begins by setting the right goals. Unfortunately, in our personal lives, goal setting is rarely done correctly.

The nation's 50 percent divorce rate suggests there are a lot of unhappy married people, many of whom believe they will be happy if only they get a divorce. In other words, getting a divorce becomes the goal. However, the even worse 60+ percent divorce rate among those marrying more than once suggests otherwise. Although they achieved their stated goal (they got divorced), happiness did not follow.

ONE NOT SO SWINGIN' SINGLE

A colleague of mine took this path. Unhappy in his marriage, he decided he would be better off as a single man. After an emotional, expensive divorce, he relocated to a singles apartment complex, complete with pool parties and opportunities for socializing. Was he happy? He seemed so.

Yet just six months after his divorce, he confided that although single life was fun at first, he no longer enjoyed it as much as he had initially, to the point of even second-guessing the wisdom of his divorce. What happened?

My friend identified divorce as a goal rather than a tactic. He did not take enough time to analyze his feelings. Although he knew he was unhappy, he assumed that getting a divorce would solve everything.

"Get a divorce" was the wrong goal. Although he and his wife did not agree about many things, their relationship was not the only or even the primary cause of his unhappiness. There were multiple issues. A more appropriate goal for him would have been to "discover the reasons for my unhappiness."

In business or at home, setting the wrong goal is the surest way to fail before you begin. What mistakes do individuals make when addressing problems? In business, management often invests significant time thinking about planning. Individuals don't spend enough time planning.

Most people would benefit tremendously by taking a thoughtful approach to planning their lives, although few do. Moreover those who are inclined to plan often focus on the finance portion to the exclusion of nearly everything else.

It's hard to blame them, really. Look for a book on personal planning, and you'll find thousands about getting your financial affairs in order versus, for example, enjoying life to the fullest. Why bother developing a financial plan that will enable you to retire at forty if you are unhappy and don't know why?

Financial planning is essential, but so is creating a life of enjoyment and fulfillment. Some do get it right, at least to a point. The questionnaire leading to the survey results discussed in chapter 1 also included an invitation to the respondents to call and talk anonymously about personal changes in their lives, and some of what they had to say clearly makes this point.

CAROL: PLANNING IS SECOND NATURE

"Carol," a fifty-eight-year-old who was job hunting, wondered if a guy writing a book about change had any suggestions for her.

At first, I assumed that she was another victim of the economy. Nearing the end of her working years, Carol was out of a job with little or no idea what to do next. No longer viewed as prime candidates by potential employers, people like her don't have the financial resources to stop working or retire.

Carol began our conversation by telling me she did not feel in control of her life. She was out of work after quitting a franchise business she bought eight years earlier. Before that, she worked for another company for ten years before being laid off.

Carol recounted her efforts to find work, including in-person and online networking. She'd taken courses to sharpen her skills and improve her résumé; attended self-help coaching classes; and even retained a life coach to help her think about her job hunting, career path, and finances. She was working hard at finding work.

I'd had conversations with others facing similar challenges, but none had been as proactive as Carol. In fact, many had not even drafted a résumé or considered networking. They were the human equivalent of a deer caught in headlights, soon to be roadkill.

Even if Carol didn't recognize it, planning was in her blood. Years earlier, she was unhappily married and concluded that her seventeen-year marriage would soon end. With that the case, she decided to prepare for life on her own and developed a plan that included returning to college to complete her bachelor's degree, followed by landing a job in marketing. After she accomplished these goals, she initiated divorce proceedings on her terms.

Twenty-three years later, Carol was not where she wanted and expected to be and was uncertain what to do next. However, even though she didn't know it, Carol had demonstrated the basic skill set necessary to move to the next phase of her life. The only thing she lacked was a clear understanding of what she wanted that next phase to be—in other words, her goals.

"I want to work, I have to work, but I don't know at what. I know I want it [to] make a difference and don't want to be on any more career ladders," she told me.

I asked her if she had a personal vision for herself, and she said, "I'm not sure, other than knowing I want it to put me around people, ideally something requiring travel."

Sound familiar? It's easy to think of the young as those searching to find themselves. But then one day it is we, now older, facing major changes, possibly recognizing our own unhappiness, feeling stuck for the rest of our lives. Not pleasant is it?

The reality is that age has little to do with knowing who we are. It's about having goals—things we really want to accomplish. Moreover, although we may achieve our goals as Carol did almost twenty-five years ago, circumstances change, so we need to adjust accordingly to move on to whatever *should* be next (which can be different from what *will* be next if we do nothing).

Carol was rightfully frustrated with not knowing what goals were important for her now, but I believe she is far better off than she assumed. She knows how to plan and has successfully executed plans in the past. All that remains is for her to determine what's next for her.

Until our phone conversation, her efforts had been centered on garnering more tools to make her more attractive to those who could offer her a position she would want to take. But now it was time for Carol to focus on the second of five reasons why change initiatives fail. She needed to decide what she wanted to change.

Business, managers, employees, you, and me—it doesn't matter. We all must decide what we want, create a plan to make it happen, and do what the plan says to do. Dysfunctional individuals, regardless of the causes, will be largely—if not completely—incapable of acting as functional employees. Although this is of concern to the individual, this should also be an equal concern for management.

You can't change "it" if you don't know what "it" is.

CHAPTER 5

The Role of Change "Triggers"

Change is inevitable, and everything changes. But what makes change happen? If we knew, we could simply watch for the causes and take the right action at the right time. Although it's not that simple, we can learn to spot the positive and negative triggers that create change in our lives.

TRIGGERS: ALL SHAPES AND SIZES

Change triggers come in two flavors: those initiated by external forces (people, circumstances, and nature) and those that are self-initiated. Both are predictable and observable when you know what to watch for.

Changes triggered by external forces include milestones, such as getting hired, promoted, demoted, or fired. In addition, you may have to adjust to your employer's challenges, such as declining markets, new competitive pressures, or even unexpected rapid growth.

Hearing your significant other announce that your relationship needs to deepen, improve, or end is certainly a trigger. So is getting a frightening medical diagnosis. And let's not forget fires, floods, hurricanes, tornadoes, earthquakes, and those other acts-of-God triggers.

Excluding weather, all these examples can be recast as self-initiated triggers. The difference is that we are initiating the change. We quit one job to take another; end or advance a relationship; or take steps to stop smoking, lose weight, or start exercising. (Unfortunately, we can also take up smoking, ditch the diet, and quit the gym. Bad triggers also happen to good people.)

WHO'S PULLING THE TRIGGER?

Whether the external or the self-initiated change trigger was expected influences the outcome…but not for the reason you'd think. If a trigger catches us by surprise, our lack of preparation means we'll be more re-active than proactive, at least at first. Clearly, self-initiated triggers can-not be completely unexpected, but the advantage of foreknowledge is lost if little or no planning is done.

Without a plan, an unexpected external trigger and an expected self-initiated trigger will result in a similar outcome: scrambling for solutions rather than acting on a carefully crafted strategy. Here's an example.

Did you ever wake up one morning and for the first time decide to find a new job that very day? Probably not. For most people, getting a new job is a process, not a single task.

What starts this process? Often, it's anticipating an external trigger, such as rumored layoffs or salary reductions, but it could also result from be-ing let go unexpectedly. Regardless, when we trigger the change our-selves, the ultimate outcome depends on what happens after we begin the process.

My consultancy keeps me in touch with hundreds of professionals, in-cluding those who can hire others, and, as a result, many of my contacts assume I can help them find new jobs when the time comes. While I like helping just for the sake of helping, I've also seen enough *Godfather* movies to know that the person I help now may help me later.

But there are limits. I have only so much relationship capital to spend, and it is not in anyone's best interest to attempt a business match that I suspect won't work.

At best, I can open a door (by making an introduction); in many cases only a crack. It's up to the job seeker to then make the most of a new connection, and many are just not prepared to do what they need to do.

LIST BEFORE YOU LEAP

Triggering a job search or a career change is not enough, and only asking for help is premature. The first step is listing and prioritizing all the steps necessary to reach your goal. Without that, outside help won't be of much use.

Take, for example, a person who decides to move. No one unexpectedly gets up one morning, packs boxes, loads the car, and drives until the right house or apartment presents itself. Instead, the process begins by this person identifying the need or the desire to make a change. His or her current home may be too big, too small, too far from work, too expensive, or other. What happens next will take time, particularly if he or she needs to wait for a lease to run out or the property to sell.

Certainly some circumstances prompt an immediate move. Should an environment or a relationship become dangerous, the only plan necessary is to make sure where you sleep tonight is somewhere other than where you slept the night before.

Of the many self-initiated change triggers, education is of greatest importance because of its potential broad and lasting impact. For most adults, pursuing education beyond high school was a decision dependent on many factors: their parents' own education, the value the family placed on education, the ability to pay for college, and the abilities or lack thereof in areas not requiring additional education.

However, returning to school later to finish college, obtain an advanced degree, or simply brush up on skills requires more thought and planning. Many individuals who self-initiated an education trigger did so with the intention of changing careers. But if you pick the wrong school, the wrong degree, or the wrong subjects, the money and time invested may not produce the desired results.

Nearly everyone has fantasized about starting a new and different career. You've read about lawyers who give up law to become teachers or novelists, or about overworked Wall Street financiers who move to New Hampshire to build furniture.

But for many, the grass is not only no greener on the other side of the fence but may also be nonexistent. Imagine earning an executive MBA and then finding out it's not the degree required by the companies you'd like to work for.

And these days, it seems everyone knows someone who obtained a real estate license to make easy money helping friends and family members buy and sell properties. They quickly learn that people they know are already being courted by newly minted realtors wanting to do the same thing.

That said, although most anyone who self-initiates an education trigger is ahead of the many who should but don't, intentions alone aren't enough. Good ideas followed by bad or no planning often yields the same disappointing result.

KNOW WHAT YOU KNOW

It's not that you must have an advanced degree from Harvard. Indeed, many people with Ivy League degrees later leave the professions they worked so hard to enter. Likewise, plenty of people who never self-initiate education triggers lead completely happy and fulfilling lives. My suggestion is only that you make these decisions as carefully and consciously as possible given all that is at stake.

Change triggers are critically important to every aspect of your life—from your financial security to your relationships, health, and well-being. And change triggers also abound at your job (even if you're self-employed); all you need do is look for them.

Before you protest that monitoring the harbingers of change at your company is not your job—or that doing so is above your pay grade—remember this: It is in your best interests to anticipate and plan for rather than react to change.

Let's look at how change triggers have impacted the lives of three people.

ALAN: RIGHT PLACE, RIGHT TIME UNTIL...

As a kid, Alan loved music, especially rock and roll. He also enjoyed the equipment that played his music at home and in his car. Alan naturally gravitated toward aftermarket car stereos, learning how to install equipment in his vehicle and in those of his friends and family.

Although intelligent and ambitious, Alan did not earn stellar grades in high school, so he decided against college. His career as a car stereo installer began in high school, first for his friends, then later as an installer at a local car stereo shop.

Alan grew up in a small town near the Oregon and California border— one of those places where everyone seems to know everyone else's business. In this community, his aptitude for car stereo installation soon made him a minor celebrity, and he received plenty of job offers. As long as he was willing to lie on the floors of vehicles to install the components, his future looked bright.

During this time, it was common for sales and marketing executives from the major car stereo manufacturers to visit car stereo shop owners to get to know the experienced installers. Eventually, some of these companies paid to fly Alan to their headquarters to participate in installer councils. At these events, top installers from across the United States would teach the manufacturers what was right and wrong with their products.

Many of these councils included Japanese executives from the parent company, and even with the language barrier, it was apparent to them that Alan knew what he was talking about. Finally, one of the leading companies offered Alan a job as in-house installation advisor.

This was a great opportunity to earn far more than the local car stereo shops could pay, so he accepted the offer and moved to his new employer's Southern California–based U.S. headquarters.

Alan was making far more money than he had ever expected and made a successful transition from his small town to a large metropolitan area. His employer flew him around the country to teach others his installation techniques. His duties soon expanded to include two or three trips a year to Japan, where his advice and expertise were in great demand by the parent company. For a guy in his late twenties with no college degree, life was good.

Alan quickly rose to the highest level in his field, but by the time he was in his early thirties, he was wondering what might be next. He enjoyed his salary and the respect of his coworkers, but he was getting tired of doing essentially the same work he did as a teenager.

Finally, Alan decided to let his boss know that he hoped there would be other opportunities in the not-too-distant future. He was especially interested in sales because of the potential for even greater compensation and because he knew sales wouldn't involve spending his days under a dashboard.

His employer did not want to lose Alan's installation expertise, but Alan emphasized that his ability to sell would be based on knowing more about installing more brands of products than any other salesperson.

Less than six months later, Alan's boss had found a new position for him. Alan would start as a sales trainee at the regional sales office, coincidentally located at the company headquarters in Southern California. Alan's boss admitted management had doubts about his sales ability and wanted to keep an eye on him. Should it turn out that he did not like sales or was not producing, his old job or something similar would be waiting for him. Alan eagerly began his sales career.

Much to everyone's delight, Alan soon exceeded his company's expectations as well as his own. Alan was a salesman! Even better, he showed signs of being a good sales manager, a rare combination among salespeople.

When shortly thereafter an assistant regional sales manager position opened in the Southeast, the company offered Alan the job. He moved to the regional sales office in Florida, and sales in his territory soon exceeded quota by 25 percent, a feat that was largely credited to Alan.

Within three years, he was offered a promotion to become the regional sales manager for the Midwest territory. Now in his late thirties, Alan was making more money than he ever thought he would. He wasn't happy about relocating to the colder Midwest, but he appreciated how lucky he was.

About this time, Alan met his future wife, June, at a trade show in Las Vegas. June also worked in the industry, although for a Korea-based company unrelated to car stereo. Unlike Alan, June was college educated with an MBA. They married a little more than a year after they met and became the parents of twin girls the following year.

June relocated to the Chicago area because they assumed Alan's job would be the basis for their future. They both wanted what was best for their children, so June quit her job. This left the couple with a reduced income that they believed they could make up with Alan's bonuses plus the part-time income June expected to generate when the girls were older.

The aftermarket car stereo industry was in a significant growth phase when Alan started working for that first retailer in his hometown some twenty years earlier, and things continued to go well for much of his career. The sound equipment installed in most new vehicles was vastly inferior to that offered by the aftermarket, and, as a result, many consumers would upgrade their vehicle sound systems.

However, much changed by the time Alan turned forty. New vehicle manufacturers had long realized that they were missing profit opportunity (and competitive advantage) by not offering better sound systems. Soon, new vehicles started shipping with quality sound equipment, and aftermarket equipment installation became more complicated because the onboard electronics were now integrated. Finally, baby boomers were aging and were no longer as interested in customizing their cars with aftermarket stereo equipment as they had in the past.

These three factors created a perfect storm for the aftermarket car stereo industry. Thus demand for the product—and therefore profits—dropped precipitously. In 2008, the U.S. economy went into its worst decline since the Great Depression, and reduced budgets and mass layoffs were common at all the major car stereo companies—Alan's included.

At forty-five years of age, Alan found himself out of a job for the first time in his life. His wife was not working, and they were raising three children. His ability or performance was never in question; the company simply needed to reduce expenses, and some top earners needed to go. Sales territories were being combined, and the company was going back to independent sales representatives. His boss told him not to worry because he was good and would find another job very quickly.

Alan was given six months separation salary plus his maximum half-year bonus. He also had his medical insurance extended during this time, all in recognition of his long service to the company. Alan realized things could be worse and indeed *were* worse for many others. So he thought, "I'll just get on with it and find another job."

As Alan quickly discovered, the poor economy meant there were many job seekers and far fewer companies that could pay for his expertise. As he worked his way through his list of contacts, he heard variations of the same thing: "I'd love to hire you, but I don't know how long I'll have a job."

Alan and June were very worried. They were one third of their way through the termination pay with nothing to show for the hundreds of résumés he had sent out. What would they do if he didn't find something soon?

At the six-month mark, Alan was drawing unemployment insurance while looking for work, but there were no opportunities in the industry he had (literally) grown up in. And no one outside the aftermarket car stereo industry was interested in talking to him because he did not have a degree.

Alan was facing a reality he had never considered. His achievements in the aftermarket industry had marked him as a "car stereo guy," someone with a very narrow and nontransferable expertise. He could go back to doing installations, but that would never pay enough to support his family. Their youngest was only seven, and although they had decided that June would be a stay-at-home mom until the kids were in high school, this was no longer an option.

Fortunately, June had an MBA and relatively recent work experience. She landed a job in Indianapolis and quickly demonstrated her value to her new employer, solidifying her position in the process.

A year passed and Alan was unable to find a new position. He was ruled out for serious consideration time and again, thanks to his lack of a college degree and the aftermarket car stereo pigeonhole.

After considering several career alternatives, Alan decided on real estate, where he could use his proven sales skills. He passed his test and went to work as a 100 percent commission agent for a local Indianapolis real estate office.

Alan quickly discovered that getting listings and selling property was not easy. Seemingly everyone he talked to already knew several real estate agents or was a weekend (i.e., part-time) agent. Plus the U.S. real estate market had suffered as much—if not more—than the overall economy. Still, Alan closed a few deals during his first year in real estate.

Alan shared all this very openly and, with his approval, has allowed me to describe his story here. Although what happened to him was specific to the aftermarket car stereo business, this general career path scenario was true for those in other fields as well. The change triggers that Alan either identified or was affected by are numerous and, in most cases, were an indication of reacting rather than being proactive.

- He (proactively) elected not to go to college even though he was intelligent enough to have done so.
- He (proactively) sought employment as a car stereo installer.
- He then (reactively) accepted a series of positions within the industry that resulted in his moving from installing car stereos to working for a car stereo manufacturer.
- He then (proactively) asked for career change to sales.

From this point on, the rest of Alan's career was reactive. His company valued him and promoted him accordingly. However, one side effect was that Alan had unknowingly let himself become a car stereo guy—one without a college degree or experience in any other industry. He became unemployable, at least at a level to which he had become accustomed.

So what could Alan have done differently? In truth, not very much. Very few people foresaw the degree to which the American economy would slide into recession. The events that unfolded over the last few years were nothing like anything any of us have experienced throughout our working careers—unlike anything since the Great Depression.

But if there was little Alan could have done to mitigate the impact on him and his family, we can certainly learn from his experience. The message is clear: Don't passively allow events to control you. If you can't determine the ultimate outcome, at least do all you can to impact the final result.

KAREN: IDENTIFY, PLAN, EXECUTE!

Karen's situation was completely different from Alan's. After graduating with a degree in sociology from Notre Dame, she accepted a position as a pharmaceutical sales representative.

We could stop right there and conclude that Karen will never experience the industry implosion that Alan did. People will always need prescription medicines, especially aging baby boomers.

Like Alan, Karen enjoyed early career success. Although she didn't relish driving from one doctor's office to the next, she was making good money doing so. Between her paycheck and college-educated husband's salary, life was good. After she and her husband, Ron, had children, Karen left her job to raise their family.

Consider Karen's triggers to this point. She was making decisions regarding her future, but all of hers were proactive rather than reactive. She decided to study a certain subject at a top college. After graduation, she chose to become a pharmaceutical sales representative. She and her husband proactively decided that she should be a stay-at-home mother to their children.

Fortunately for Karen, Ron's income allowed her to remain home even longer than the couple envisioned. After leaving her pharmaceutical job, Karen did not work outside the home for twenty-three years. But at fifty-one years of age, with all the kids out of the house, Karen decided it was time to find something else to do, with the only question being, what would that be?

The pharmaceutical sales job was fine for a recent college graduate, but she didn't want to do that now. Sociology was out because she did not have an advanced degree or interest in graduate school. Although Karen knew companies would value her bachelor's degree, her education and skills were out of date compared to more recent college graduates.

She had always been drawn to technology. Her husband had an

engineering degree, but it was Karen who was fascinated with computing, home audio equipment, and televisions. In short, any technology that was new and different.

She began to wonder about a second career in computer programming. Could she attend trade school to learn marketable computer programming skills? Although still far from retirement, Karen wanted to avoid working over sixty hours a week or even forty hours if possible. Could she be a part-time computer programmer?

After researching her options, Karen settled on a trade school that offered a programming curriculum that seemed to meet her needs, a decision she did not make lightly. She polled people on the value of such a program, particularly for a fifty-one-year-old woman. Predictably, the responses she received reflected the circumstances of those offering the feedback.

She had many women friends who had also raised children. Some had degrees and some didn't. Some had no intention of working, whereas others had worked during or after their kids were grown. They either agreed with her plan or told her she was making a big mistake. Karen knew she needed to talk to others, specifically, those who would consider hiring her in the future.

She contacted personnel departments at companies she thought might be interested in her after she finished her technical training. What she found was eye opening.

Given her age and lack of full-time availability, she would not be a top candidate. Too many hungry new college graduates in their early twenties were ready to snap up the openings.

But more than one personnel manager suggested she contact outsourcing companies who provide part-time help for companies such as theirs. These companies supplied workers for overflow situations, where the workload was predictable in length and always temporary.

What she discovered about the outsourcing companies was very encouraging. Her age would not be a factor. Part-time work is exactly what they had to offer, and they had hired many trade school graduates with great success.

Karen was sold. She enrolled and completed the course in less than eighteen months. She said she found the programming courses to be exhilarating and was eager to start working. The outsourcing company she now works for recognized that Karen had the right combination of qualities. She was well trained, dependable, and realistic in her expectations for compensation. She had all the work she wanted.

Karen was a few months short of her fifty-ninth birthday when she told me her story while happily working an average of three days a week. Her husband's plan was to retire in two years, at which time she would retire as well, allowing them to travel and enjoy their postcareer lives as they had always planned to do.

So what about Karen's triggers after she decided to stay at home and raise her children? True to form she continued to be proactive, thinking ahead, doing what she thought she wanted compared with simply reacting as Alan had often done. Karen was also very proactive in her approach to her second career. She didn't simply decide she wanted to be a computer programmer; she sought opinions from others whose knowledge she valued, and when the advice coming from friends and family was mixed, she broadened her approach and sought the advice of experts—the very people she would expect to hire her as a programmer.

Whether Karen retires when her husband does or not, whatever she elects to do will likely be the result of great thought and planning. She will almost certainly continue to identify and act on her change triggers as she has in the past.

SYBIL: FACING THE MUSIC

Sybil, thirty-seven years old, is an unmarried, self-proclaimed bisexual woman. Like Karen, Sybil completed my survey and then called to talk regarding changes in her life. Her story is not any more or less interesting than Alan's or Karen's, but her experience has been different.

Like Alan, Sybil also enjoyed music from a very early age, teaching herself to play guitar and singing while in her teens. She also decided not to attend college because she wanted to pursue a career as a professional musician.

At first, she would play most anywhere an audience could be found, including coffee houses, bars, restaurants, and sometimes even on the street in her hometown. This was all good fun, she told me, because she was living as she imagined singers/songwriters like Bob Dylan and Joan Baez had done in the early stages of their careers.

The life of an itinerant musician may be an adventure in one's twenties, but Sybil soon realized it would be less fun as she got older. She decided it was time to amend her dream. This meant finding a job that would allow her to continue her pursuit of a music career while at the same time providing steady income.

Like Karen, Sybil talked to friends and family members before deciding to apply to become a flight attendant. Although free travel was a bonus, for Sybil the primary attraction was working just a few days a week with the rest of her time devoted to music.

Sybil was hired by United Airlines and began her career flying to destinations assigned to those with lower seniority. So her time off was not spent in New York, Miami, and Los Angeles. Instead, Sybil often found herself spending the night in Indianapolis, St. Louis, and other Midwest destinations. But she was free to use her time off playing guitar and singing.

Up to this point, Sybil's change triggers were somewhat closer to Alan's than to Karen's. Unlike Alan, Sybil had been more proactive in her choices, deciding to become a flight attendant to solve her income problem yet still have time to pursue music. However, she had another goal, and it was at odds with her career. She wanted to be in a stable relationship. "It never even crossed my mind that living the life I had chosen might rule out ever meeting somebody I could get close to," she told me.

Although she had been proactive in identifying and achieving some of her goals, she had failed to think through the implications of her decisions relative to her personal life. So, in her late thirties, she once again decided to make a change.

As had Karen, Sybil thought about what she should do to create a more well-rounded future for herself; one that would provide sufficient income while at the same time allowing her to pursue her music career.

And she would also concentrate more on developing a relationship with someone she cared for.

After much thought, Sybil decided that she could accomplish all this by reversing her focus on income first and music second by playing more than just local venues near where she lived in New Hampshire. After quitting her job at United Airlines, she relocated to Manchester, New Hampshire, and using that as a base, began playing in local clubs throughout New England.

Soon she was meeting or exceeding her salary as a flight attendant while spending far less time traveling to gigs. Being a flight attendant had required her to be away for several days each week. When "home," she could spend a few more days and evenings playing in clubs. Now she was in effect combining the two, traveling less, and leaving the balance of the week to build her personal life in Manchester.

Unlike many musicians, Sybil was not a drinker, not even socially, and she had never smoked, knowing it would harm her singing voice. She wanted to meet someone with similar habits and values, but she spent a lot of time in clubs and bars playing for crowds that consisted mostly of smokers and drinkers—who were by now a lot younger than her.

Working as a flight attendant and spending weekends playing music made staying fit difficult. Although she was not overweight, she told me she was "not in great shape," so fitness was added to her list of goals. She joined a gym, which improved her health, and let her work out in the company of the kind of people she wanted to meet. Few were drinkers or smokers. They were people concerned about their health, and along with those she met while jogging, playing tennis, and golf, her choice of people she might like to have a relationship with increased significantly.

Sybil soon met a woman only a few years older than her whose beliefs and sexual orientation were similar to hers. However, there was a major stumbling block. Her new friend did not like Sybil spending most weekends away, playing and singing. Six months later, the woman made it clear that either Sybil's priorities needed to change or their relationship would end.

Sybil was once again at a crossroads. She was making a living, doing what she enjoyed, and had even managed to meet someone with whom she thought she might like to spend the rest of her life. The problem was that her girlfriend's change triggers, priorities, and goals were different from Sybil's.

After much consideration, Sybil decided it was time to make another change. Although she enjoyed performing, she didn't love it enough to justify giving up her relationship. So she stopped accepting engagements outside of Manchester.

Although this solved one problem, it created another. Her income had, in part, depended on traveling to perform, so she was once again forced to reconsider her employment options. But now she would take her new relationship into consideration and attempt to achieve balance.

When I last talked with Sybil, she had found what she believes to be the best possible solution. Although she still performs locally, mostly on weekends, she now teaches singing and guitar at a local music store during the day. She has enough time to continue her quest to be physically fit and further her relationship. All things considered, she said, life was good.

WHO ARE YOU?

Consider the stories of Alan, Karen, and Sybil. Alan is clearly someone who mostly reacts to external change triggers, whereas Karen is almost the exact opposite, being very proactive and deciding which triggers she will respond to and how. And then there is Sybil who, like most of us most of the time, is somewhere in between.

Whatever your situation, you can learn from Alan, Karen, and Sybil. You are much further ahead the more proactive you are, the more you initiate and define the change triggers that will guide your life, and, as with these three, it is never to late to start.

Occasionally take a look at your career, particularly if you are in your twenties or thirties. If you continue to work in one industry and certainly within one company within that industry, you run the risk of being permanently identified with that type of work. If your industry takes a hit, so do you.

As you consider your career triggers, think as much about ten, fifteen, or twenty years from now as you do today. Although you do not want to pass up a short-term opportunity, you also want to make decisions today that will be in your best interests in the future.

CHAPTER 6

A Memo to Management

The 7 Keys to Change was written to help individuals bring about positive changes in their lives, including job performance. However, there are also lessons for the managers among you. Indeed, the degree to which your employees can improve their ability to manage change will directly impact your business. The better your employees successfully manage change at home, the fewer personal problems they will bring to work, and the better equipped they will be to carry out the company's change initiatives.

Although each person needs to solve his or her own problems, you can and should take steps to support your employees. Why? Let's revisit the one statistic that should provide the most motivation: Almost two out of three corporate change initiatives fail.

Thousands of books and articles describe the importance of planning and change management, with most of them telling managers what change management is and how to do it. The one thing the majority agrees on is the need for employee buy-in. Few managers would dispute this because without employees, nothing gets done—including change initiatives. Why not do all you can then to help your employees help you?

WHY THEIR PROBLEMS ARE YOUR PROBLEMS

Just as the advice to individuals is to first recognize their obligation to themselves to proactively attempt to manage change in their lives, you need to understand that without optimum participation from your employees, your change initiatives will all too often fail.

If you secretly believe you can force change or find employees who share your views, prepare for a big disappointment. Often, the problem is not that individuals are incapable of accomplishing certain tasks, but they are prevented from succeeding because neither they nor their managers understand the blocks that prevent them from being more effective.

The second requirement is recognizing that each employee has a vastly different level of understanding of what it means to manage change. This results in a variety of efforts working at cross-purposes.

Finally, of greatest importance, the personal issues of employees rightfully take center stage in their lives and can distract their focus on business. This more than anything could be enough to block their efforts on behalf of the company.

IT'S ALWAYS PERSONAL

Often, an otherwise good employee, one who has repeatedly demonstrated an ability to do his or her job, is not necessarily going to be effective participating in company change initiatives. The reasons range from a lack of understanding the process to distracting personal issues. Whatever the cause, he or she cannot contribute to the change process as much as you need and wish them to do.

Some managers have trouble accepting this because they expect others to behave as they believe they do. However, although you may be able to put your personal problems aside at work, most cannot. We all deal with many of the same issues and are sometimes confronted by major challenges and tragedies. I have never met a manager who was so personally disciplined as to be able to ignore these distractions, performing at a constant high level no matter what was going on at home.

However, even if you are the exception to the rule, do not make the mistake of believing that those you manage are that way as well. Their personal issues absolutely will affect their performance and, as a result, the company as well.

I've had this discussion with many managers and find it to be one of the more difficult concepts for them to accept. If they don't offer variations of *"I deal with my problems, and they should too,"* the response is often *"Our human resources department is here to help them, and there's nothing more I can do."*

That may be true in some cases but not all, and when it's not, the outcome will be the same. You will be part of the 60 percent not achieving your objectives.

WILL YOU HELP?

As a manager, deciding to help your employees is a critical first step, but soon after, you must identify what problem you are attempting to solve, a requirement that is often easier to acknowledge than fulfill.

Psychology Today published the results of an American Psychiatric Association survey of 1,129 workers in which significant numbers of employees indicated that their employers would not respond favorably to a request for help with serious but all too common problems. As a result, 76 percent say they will not mention drug addictions, 73 percent will not discuss alcoholism, and 62 percent will not discuss issues relating to depression to their employers.[23]

As this survey shows, if helping employees is a priority, the first step is gaining their trust. Even if your company has the resources to help its workers, and regardless of whether you feel employee problems are your concern, know this: Unresolved employee problems will quite often prevent the positive changes you seek to make.

After you recognize the existence of your employees' concerns, consider engaging independent, professional help for your staff if your company does not have the internal resources necessary to help.

Finally, no matter how many college graduates and MBAs you employ, no matter how extensive their experiences in planning and change initiatives, do not assume that they are of one mind. A review of the literature addressing planning and change management, along with a cursory review of college courses addressing both, highlights why we have so much diverse opinion and misuse of planning and change initiative elements in business. Much has been written, but it's not coming from the same place.

There is considerable room for interpretation, which should alert you to the fact that although most know it is important to plan and manage change, what that is and how best to go about it varies widely. This fact, coupled with the reality that many of your employees have had little to no exposure to any of this, accounts for much of your failed change initiatives.

MAKE OR BREAK

As much as you might wish otherwise, when it comes to the personal and professional lives of your employees, there is very little—if any—separation of church and state. As a result, a problem at home will very often create or, at the very least, make worse a problem at work. Although you may not be equipped to deal with the personal issues of your employees, you ignore them at your own risk. It is better that you acknowledge that these issues exist and do whatever possible to account for them in your business, rather than fail to recognize how much they can make or break your change initiative efforts.

It's not easy, is it? In his book *EPIC Change: How to Lead Change in the Global Age*, Timothy R. Clark summarized the challenges of change management leadership quite well: "Change can be mystifying. We can't deny its complexity. It's not simple, linear, tidy, or mechanistic, and there is virtually nothing elegant about leading it."[24]

CHAPTER 7

A Letter to You

The titles of this chapter and the last highlight the differences between business and personal thinking when it comes to change. Business views itself as neat, compartmentalized, precise, and nearly scientific; hence, those involved in business would expect to be addressed in a nonpersonal memo. Interestingly, then, away from work, many of these same individuals would find it odd to receive such a memo. Instead, any communication intended for them at home would more appropriately be informal, possibly a letter but certainly not a memo.

This book addresses both business and personal perspectives because when it comes to change, they are irrevocably linked. Fortunately, the actions needed to successfully manage change in business are not at all different from those required for personal change, a few terms and mechanics notwithstanding.

So this "letter" is addressed to individuals. This book is meant to teach you what you need to do to help create more positive change in your life, including your life at work. It does not matter what you do for a living, whether you are management or even work in business. In a perfect world, a memo to management would not need to be immediately followed by a letter to you. However, the perceived differences between the two are so ingrained in our thinking as to be important in a book addressing change for both.

That said, what should you do to help create more positive change in your life?

The seventh key in Part II, which addresses attitude, says that no matter how well you understand the mechanics of planning and change management, the wrong attitude will diminish or even eliminate your ability to bring about meaningful change. Although understanding planning and change management is very important, if you did nothing beyond improving your attitude, you would be much better off. But if you are serious about bringing positive change into your life, start by familiarizing yourself with planning elements and terms and then moving on to develop a foundation of understanding for change management.

This book provides you with most of what you need to know, but if you can, continue your education with one or more of the many excellent books addressing planning and change management that go into greater detail. Read a few, learn from them, and, of greatest importance, begin to apply the techniques they teach you at home and at work.

A WORD OF CAUTION

If you spend any time reading about planning and talking to those involved with it, you will soon realize that there is an ongoing debate about the meaning of each critical term as well as how to use them. If we were dealing with mathematics, science, or a foreign language, I would recommend taking the time to learn the right term for the right situation. But this is not so for planning. For unknown reasons, the business world employs precise-sounding terms in a variety of ways. Meanings may differ from company to company or even department to department, creating confusion among those involved with planning.

So what can you do? Work to gain a foundational understanding of terms such as vision, vision statement, mission, mission statement, strategies, goals, objectives, and tactics. But also know that the strong opinions of those who use these terms notwithstanding, there is no well-established agreed-on definition for each. Feel free to co-opt the definitions that work best for your situation and leave the rest behind, including the seemingly endless definition debate. In other words, don't get hung up on planning jargon that will likely never be resolved, which will have little to do with your ultimate success.

BEYOND SEMANTICS

After you understand the process and get past the terms debate, you reach the most critical element of the planning process. You must decide what you want to change, what you want to happen, and what you want to become. The reason this is so important should be obvious; if you do not correctly identify your goals or objectives (let's not debate the difference between the two), although you may achieve what you set out to do, what that is may not be what you really want or need.

Many establish the wrong objectives, only to find that after the goal has been reached, the desired outcome was not as expected. Beyond unfortunate, this is giant waste of time and often requires starting over or, worse, accepting that your true desired goals are now unattainable. Fortunately, you can avoid this by taking the time to really understand what you want to accomplish before planning anything.

Most people understand that change in business comes only from a well-organized, well-motivated team effort. However, enlisting help from others is no less important when attempting to bring about change in our personal lives.

When considering personal change, you would do well to recognize that meaningful change will require help and assistance from others, in addition to all that you have to do on your own. Many personal change initiatives involve sensitive or potentially embarrassing situations that could become even more uncomfortable by discussing them with others. Nonetheless, doing so is an important requirement for success.

YOUR OWN WORST ENEMY

Up to this point, the discussion has addressed only the mechanical elements. However, the "you" must be considered in all this as well. You may know what to do and still fail because, as strange as it may seem, you stood in your own way, preventing your success. Often, people fail to bring about change in their lives because of a certain mind-set, which, in turn, governs all other elements in their approach to change.

The more I think about it, the less certain I am about how easy or difficult this is to address. Although I consider myself to be a focused, self-directed person, I've occasionally had difficulty adjusting and controlling my thinking and emotions. Often, it is much easier to help someone else do that than it is to do it for ourselves, but that is what we must do nonetheless.

The best advice I can give you is to recognize that the single greatest obstacle to your success is likely you. How you think, your attitude, and the stumbling blocks you create will have much to do with your ability to achieve your goals. Do not underestimate your own ability to take yourself out of the game. If you can legitimately gain support in your change effort, you will have done much toward reaching your goals. As so many self-help books do, I'd like to say "You can do it," but that is almost entirely up to you.

Accept that no matter how significant or insignificant your goals, learning the processes necessary to bring about positive change is itself a life-changing event. Although you may be considering a relatively minor change, such as moving a short distance or considering additional education, the day will come when the stakes will be much higher. So learn the processes now, "off-Broadway" so to speak, with change initiatives less critical than some of the major ones that you'll undoubtedly face in the future.

Finally, I want to circle back to the relationship between you as an individual and the companies that employ you. With few exceptions, most of what I found regarding change treated business and personal change as completely separate subjects. They are, in fact, completely related. Both management and employees are irrevocably linked in their successes and failures. Embrace this common need for each other and work for the mutual benefit of both. When it comes to change, whether it is business or personal, there is no separation of church and state. Your fates are one and the same.

PART II
Getting Good at Change:
Seven Keys to Get Where You Want to Be

KEY #1

The Inevitable Change:
You Couldn't Stop It Even If You Wanted To

"Most of us are about as eager to be changed as we were to be born, and go through our changes in a similar state of shock."—James Baldwin[25]

If you could change one thing about your life, what would it be? Think carefully.

That question makes me consider many aspects of my life, including my finances, my health, my relationships, my career, where I live, how I spend my work and recreation time, and so on. It's that way for most of us. Very few people look back and see nothing that could be changed for the better. However, if you're one of the very few who see nothing to change, congratulations on a successful life! But for the rest of us, there are things we would have done differently, and there will be more in the future as well.

So, "If you could change one thing about your life, what would it be?" is a trick question, with the best answer being, "I want to change the way I handle change—to learn how to do it better."

Think about it. For me, everything listed here involved good or bad change. I made more money and sometimes less. I have had a few bad relationships but many good. For the most part, I have been quite healthy but not always. I've given good advice to people asking for my help, although sometimes not the best advice. Everything about my life, absolutely everything, has change at its core, and that will continue to be true well past the day I die (because what I have done with my life will continue to affect many others long after I'm gone).

And guess what? You and everyone who has ever lived have the same reality at the center of your life—change.

You might think I'm overstating this point, that I feel this way after investing four years of research into the subject. However, having done so, I clearly see the importance of everything that improves our ability to deal with change. Still not convinced? Think about it some more.

Like it or not, most agree that change is inevitably, immeasurably important, affecting everything in our lives every day. Also, change comes in two flavors: unexpected or unplanned and anticipated or planned. Actually, I should say, "hopefully planned" because people often anticipate and initiate change without any preparation at all. Remember, I'm a planning consultant, one biased toward planning, but that aside, the following example should convince you of its importance.

THE (NOT NEARLY ENOUGH) PLANNED TRIP

Let's say I want to go from the West Coast to the East Coast. Most of us contemplating such a trip would not simply get up one morning and head east. Instead, we determine that we want to depart from one city (e.g., Los Angeles) and arrive in another (e.g., New York City), a decision that becomes the first glimmer of a plan.

Many activities do not require extremely detailed planning, and this trip from Los Angeles to New York may well be one of them. We often conduct preliminary planning almost unconsciously. If I need to travel from Los Angeles to New York City, I have already worked out the vision or reason I am going.

Likewise, I don't need to spend much time articulating my travel strategy; the default choice is typically a commercial airline. However, there are alternatives. I could drive to New York City, I could take a bus, I could go by train, or I could even travel by ship down the West Coast to Central America, passing through the Panama Canal, sailing north up the eastern coastline, eventually arriving in New York City. Do I need to spend time contemplating the positives and negatives of each alternative? No, I instantly know that the right option is a five-hour commercial flight.

But not everything about this trip is certain, and if I don't do some planning, I increase the chances of something going wrong.

The reason for my trip is the need to introduce my company to a new prospective client, so, I must get to New York City as soon as possible.

So I go online and buy a ticket from Los Angeles International Airport to John F. Kennedy Airport, leaving at 8:30 a.m. the next day. I pack my suitcase, thinking about my needs for the trip, including duration, weather, and how formal I expect the client will be. My suitcase packed, my presentation on my computer, I can relax for the night.

Around 10 p.m., I go to bed after setting my alarm for 5 a.m. After a good night's sleep, I shower, dress, eat, and leave for the airport by 6 a.m. Unexpected traffic eats up half an hour. Hmm, I hadn't anticipated that, and if I encounter long security lines at the airport, I may miss my flight. This could potentially be a major problem because I have assured my prospect that I will arrive at 9 a.m. sharp the next day.

Take a deep breath. I can catch a later flight if necessary, although that means I won't have the luxury of relaxing in New York City the night before the meeting.

Phew! The security lines are not too bad, and I make my flight, which arrives in New York City a mere twenty minutes after the estimated arrival time. I take the train into the city and arrive at my hotel just a little more than an hour after I had assumed I would. So far, so good.

After a good meal and a restful night, I awake thinking about how to impress this prospective client. I leave the hotel, walk three blocks to the client's office, and arrive fifteen minutes early.

An administrative assistant takes me to the conference room where I connect my laptop to the client's overhead projector. I'm thinking about the amount of effort I put into my PowerPoint presentation. Everything is riding on it. I have practiced and believe I'm ready, but you never know for sure until you begin the presentation. The client walks in, greets me, takes a seat, and says her time is limited.

It's go time! And then it hits me. I forgot my laptop's power adapter. Now what? My presentation is long. What if it's so long my laptop's battery dies in the middle? What if the battery lasts but the prospect loses interest? Or runs out of time?

Then my thoughts became more accusatory: "If only I had given more thought to the details, this never would have happened. If I had just spent more time planning the specifics…."

Before the trip, I saw no need to formally plan for all eventualities that could impact the outcome. My potential presentation pitfall (the battery survived the presentation) happened because I allowed myself to be subjected to unanticipated change rather than doing all I could to anticipate and proactively manage events.

BEEN THERE, DONE THAT

If your work involves making presentations, you likely have a few presentation war stories of your own. If not, you may think this one has nothing to do with you. Think again. Remember vacations where the weather caught you by surprise, you did not allow enough time for the activities you wanted to do, or you forgot essential clothing?

Planning comes into play in everyday life. Trips to the grocery store take longer and cost more without a plan (i.e., a shopping list). Ever purge your messy garage only to soon find that you need one of the items you threw away? Forgetting the milk or rebuying a discarded gadget is minor annoyance but are you willing to forgo planning when it comes to the matters that concern you most?

Whether pitching new business in New York, considering a job change, relocating to a new city, pursuing further education, or beginning or ending a relationship, overplanning is nearly impossible. The more you plan for all likely eventualities, the better the results. Carpenters summarize it best: "Measure twice, cut once."

Approaching change in a more efficient, thoughtful way is in your best interests. You'll enjoy financial rewards, enjoy better relationships, and experience fewer unexpected crises with dire consequences. Things will turn out better when you control change compared with allowing change to control you, both in your professional and personal lives.

Think about this last point and what it may mean in light of what your employer wants and expects from you. Many believe they trade hours for pay when working for someone else, so all they owe an employer is time. A smaller but still significant group assumes employers pay for performance, so doing well means raises and job security.

Don't bet on it. Prior to the 2008 financial crisis, otherwise responsible, productive people held millions of jobs that are now gone. Relatively few of those individuals lost their jobs because they didn't put in enough hours or because their performance ratings dropped. They lost their jobs because their companies could no longer afford to pay them.

So what do employers pay for? Just like you, they must see positive return on their investment (the money they pay their employees). Just like you, they must continually accomplish positive results because, as Charles Darwin's evolution postulations suggested, when businesses cease to be responsive to change, they cease to exist. (And when companies go out of business, jobs disappear.)

You alone cannot protect your job by simply doing your part to deliver positive change. But the more proactive you and your fellow employees are regarding change, the higher the likelihood your company and your jobs will continue. And should your employer not appreciate your effort, go where you will be appreciated and better compensated for your ability to bring about positive change.

Very few of us have been adequately trained in change management; however, fortunately, we can learn. Change is inevitable, but the outcome is not. Read on.

KEY #2

The Myths and Facts Surrounding Business and Personal Change

Personal change aside for the moment, what could be mythical about business change? Taken literally, mythical and myth are misleading terms, but I use them to stress that many significant assumptions regarding change are simply not true. Moreover, these untruths are harmful and often a major obstacle when attempting to bring about positive business and personal change. So what are these myths?

1. Business change always involves more than one person, whereas personal change does not.

2. Personal change is about one's mental state and life aspirations, whereas business change is grounded in business. (Here, "business" is an abstract concept that is separate and apart from people.)

3. Business planning goals are often apparent to many, whereas individual targets for change (e.g., relationships, health, and finances) are generally not discussed with others.

4. One's personal life should not intrude on the company. Personal issues must be left at home.

5. Management generally does not inquire about personal issues and problems affecting employees because they respect their

privacy.

6. Business transcends any individual; it is about the company rather than any individual or groups of individuals.

7. Because of the first six, the process one should use to make business change happen is not at all similar or certainly the same as what one should do to bring about personal change.

Before we consider each of these, think about this.

WHAT A DIFFERENCE A DAY MAKES

Assume you work for company A, which employs one hundred people. Fifteen minutes before quitting time on Monday, the CEO informs all the employees that they are not to come in on Tuesday nor do anything on Tuesday that would relate to the company's business or their jobs. No e-mail, phone calls, texting, meetings, or travel—absolutely no activities that relate to company A's business. The employees are told they can do whatever they want on Tuesday as long as it has nothing to do with work. Everyone will be paid for the day off and will be expected to return Wednesday morning as usual.

How much progress will company A make toward its planning goals or any major change initiatives during one full day without employees? Clearly, the answer is none: no employees, no progress. This may be obvious, but think about what this means.

Many managers talk about their companies as if they were separate entities, independent of employees. Although companies continue to operate in spite of turnover and retirement in the employee ranks, this does not mean a company has a life of its own. Goals are accomplished through employee actions.

The emphasis is purposeful because the foundation of many of these myths is a belief that a company transcends the people who work for it; the individual does not matter. Few responsible managers would agree that this harsh statement reflects their feelings; however, words and deeds are often at cross-purposes. If you are management, before you (too) quickly decide these statements do not describe your company, look at the difference between what your company does and what it says.

So let's consider each myth separately.

ALL FOR ONE AND ONE FOR ALL

Business change always involves more than one person, whereas personal change does not.

When I began this project, I, in part, assumed this statement was true because I had never been in a business situation where significant change was the responsibility of just one person. Indeed, often a typical first step in creating change is to appoint a committee to direct the effort.

I had decades of experience working for larger companies, including, later, consulting for large organizations. In every one of those situations, change was the responsibility of many, not one.

The only exceptions occurred during the launch of my own companies when, early on, I believed I was alone. In retrospect, I clearly see that even then that wasn't the case. I felt there was no one to turn to, but I was wrong. Although the "company" consisted of only me, I relied on my bank, an accountant, a stable of freelance consultants, and even the staff at the local copy center. Nonetheless, I did not believe this was the case for personal change. That was business, and (I thought) the rules did not apply apart from business.

When I considered the many personal changes someone might want to make—for example, losing weight, dealing with an addiction, looking for a new job, addressing relationship issues, considering a move— I believed an individual was on his or her own. Now I clearly see that is not the case. If it were true, little would get done.

If you doubt this, consider the difficulty of losing fifty, twenty, or even ten pounds. Even if you don't have a weight problem, you likely know someone who does and can understand the seemingly insurmountable challenges he or she faces.

Still, many people are successful losing weight. The difference is that few of those who reach their weight loss goals do so alone. They rely on the advice of a doctor, enroll in a weight-loss program, enlist a trainer, receive support from friends and family, or all the above.

Likewise, it's very difficult for someone to overcome substance abuse alone. Whether the addiction is to alcohol, drugs, or nicotine, success is often a combination of personal resolve coupled with external resources, such as Alcoholics Anonymous and other such groups. Those who believe they have addressed these problems alone may be overlooking the contributions of those around them.

Now I not only no longer believe that personal change is the responsibility of only one person, but I am also convinced that even the assumption that this is true is detrimental to the success of both individuals, and, by extension, the companies they work for.

A HARD LINE ON THE SOFT VIEW

Personal change is about one's mental state and life aspirations, whereas business change is grounded in business. (Here, "business" is an abstract concept that is separate and apart from people.)

This second myth points to the "soft" way we view personal issues. Business goals (we say) are real and tangible, whereas personal change is more touchy/feely. Business books are generally written by people in business for people in business, and when nonbusiness writers address businesspeople, they often change their tone accordingly.

On the other hand, authors targeting individuals do so on a much more personal level, employing more encouraging language rather than that used in business writing.

If either approach worked in all situations, we'd have a better track record for facilitating business and personal change. Sadly, we do not.

In the beginning, I was not interested in individual change and steered clear of self-help books. But after I considered the effect of personal problems on individuals/employees and, in turn, on companies, I began to realize how completely interdependent they are. There is no other way to put it; little or no significant business change can occur without the active support of the individual.

SHHH! WE DON'T TALK ABOUT THAT!

Business planning goals are often apparent to many, whereas individual targets for change (e.g., relationships, health, and finances) are generally not discussed with others.

The third myth has to do with the obviousness—or lack thereof—of business and personal goals.

Technically, this is not a myth in the sense that it is a falsehood believed by many. It's more a statement of a reality that is detrimental to both individuals and their employers. If we believe that business goals are easy to perceive and personal goals are not, the negative effect is as great as if it were a myth.

Most of us have worked with people who had significant personal issues, and while talking to them about those problems is rare, talking about them is not (gossip being an entirely different matter.)

Whether it's a coworker with the obvious drinking or drug problem; the woman clearly suffering from physical spousal abuse; or all the stories regarding pending divorce, difficulty with children, or financial trouble, we know about it, and management often does too. But knowing about problems and attempting to do something about them are two very different things, which brings us to the next two myths.

PERSONAL VERSUS PERSONNEL

One's personal life should not intrude on the company. Personal issues must be left at home.

This fourth myth holds that one's personal life should not be allowed to impact the company, and all things personal must go no further than the parking lot.

This traditional segregation of home and work started long ago when employers discouraged fraternization among employees. But it didn't end there. Long before the military's former "don't ask, don't tell" policy, management made it clear that it did not want to deal with employee problems. As a result, some companies that refer to their workers as family may be "talking the talk" while not necessarily "walking the walk."

However, to be fair, few firms have the resources or understanding required to effectively deal with the myriad of personal problems of their employees. As a result, the standard reaction is to act as if these problems do not exist.

Unfortunately, this does not work, and the result is a sizable, unrecognized cost associated with goals missed due to employee problems. Which takes us to the next myth addressing the chasm been home and work.

THE "NONE OF MY BUSINESS" BUSINESS

Management generally does not inquire about personal issues and problems affecting employees because they respect their privacy.

For the most part, management correctly understands it is not prepared to help, including lacking critical resources necessary to address employee personal issues. And even if that weren't true, management may not be willing to accept the potential liability associated with a failed attempt.

Instead, there is an informal—if not formal—"firewall" between management and employee personal lives, leaving it to the individuals to handle their personal issues, expecting them to be effective in their jobs no matter what goes on outside the company. Some do or are capable of hiding their personal problems, appearing to function as expected, but not all are capable of this.

Staying within the confines of employment law, companies will do what they can to help their employees; however, when issues become serious enough to negatively affect performance, the result is often dismissal. The cost to the individual is obvious: lost income as well as the stigma associated with being terminated. There is also a significant but not always recognized cost to the company in the form of missed company goals (remember that 60 percent figure).

All these myths bring us to the sixth misconception, which, on some levels, is understandable and, to a point, even defensible.

IT'S ABOUT US, NOT YOU!

Business transcends any individual; it is about the company rather than any individual or groups of individuals.

Companies often outlive most if not all their employees, so it would be easy to assume that a company exists in spite of turnover. However, as the example of company A demonstrated, we must never forget that there is no company if there are no employees—or when employees are no longer effective.

THE "THAT'S NOT HOW I DO IT" MYTH

Because of the first six, the process one should use to make business change happen is not at all similar or certainly the same to what one should do to bring about personal change.

As the survey results in chapter 1 showed, many people don't know whether this is true or not. Does it matter whether these processes are the same or similar? Yes, it does matter.

If the processes were not the same, everyone would have to learn two change systems: one for business and one for their personal lives. This, in turn, would increase confusion resulting from individual employees doing bits and pieces of whatever system they use for personal change, just as happens when managers apply their own interpretations of the change process.

Fortunately, the change process for individuals and business is not significantly different; a conclusion also reached by Dr. Sylvia LaFair, who said, "The overriding idea is that the process of breaking through barriers in the workplace is nearly identical to the process of doing it with your family."[26]

ARE WE BLIND?

So what prevents others from seeing this? The answer is related to the earlier cited reasons having to do with why change initiatives so often fail. They fail, in part, because the change process is simply not well understood.

Change management and even business planning are not core requirements in all business degrees, and neither skill is typically taught to middle or senior managers. Instead, senior management simply assumes its employees and certainly its managers know what to do. Unfortunately, this doesn't happen as often or as consistently as is desirable.

Complicating things, many managers do not understand the correlation between the personal problems of their employees and their ineffective participation in change initiatives at work. The corporate firewall between personal and professional lives renders us largely incapable of recognizing the interdependency of both.

And, by the way, this "gate" also swings both ways. Although I have never seen statistics showing how many marriages or parenting relationships have been damaged as the result of work pressure, most of us can provide anecdotal evidence that it does happen. And the reverse scenario is possible as well, with personal problems adversely affecting work performance.

Finally, there is the effect of self-fulfilling prophecy. We respond to what we know or what we believe we know. The fact that we believe these myths causes us to act on them, which, in turn, reinforces our belief that they are true. Management can address this by looking at how the organization sees each point; if it doesn't, you can and should do that for yourself.

WE ARE FAMILY?

Before leaving the myths discussion, let's briefly reflect on the meaning of some of the survey results included in chapter 1—in this case, those having to do with companies telling their employees they are family. As a reminder, these data came from over 500 randomly selected individuals, including many similar to you, and you might well find yourself reflected in their answers. But of greater importance, think about what this means to both your personal and business lives.

Nothing points to the uncertainly in people's minds regarding what to do about change in their business and personal lives than does the answer to the following question: "Is the process people should use to change things in their business lives the same or similar to what they should do to change things in their personal lives?" Almost one third of the respondents believed it is the same or similar, with an almost equal number saying it is not; the remainder, not sure.

Employers, do you still think your employees are on the same page when it comes to knowing how they can contribute to making positive change happen in your business? Remember, no matter how they answered this question, that doesn't mean that what they think they should do is what you want or need them to do.

Similarly, if you're a member of the "not sure" group, rest assured that many of the two thirds who indicated they knew actually did not. I found this to be true numerous times in the one-on-one follow-up conversations when asking "What is the process?" from both those who said it is the same as well as those who said it isn't. If we can't agree on whether there is single process for changing our personal and business lives, can you imagine how difficult it will be to reach agreement on the process itself?

The questions addressing how much or how little employees believe their companies include them and their actual families as part of a company family also point to interesting possible conclusions. However, we first must acknowledge that no organization is obligated to think of its employees as family or, if it does, to include the employee's family in that consideration. Nor is there anything inherently right or wrong in what an organization does. The point of these questions is only to gain insight concerning how individuals perceive their employer's concern for them and their families—and then only for a secondary reason.

You might feel good when your company says they care about you, and you might feel even better if they include your family. However, if the company's actions do not align with its words, any potential benefit is lost. And employers, what do you think happens when your employees conclude that what management says is not what it does? How much effort on behalf of the company can you reasonably expect from your employees when your words and actions don't align?

The data showed that although one third of companies describe themselves as family oriented, only 6 percent of employees feel that company actions match their words. In anyone's book, this is a major credibility gap.

Companies are not doing all they should to connect their employees to their businesses, for not only the employee's benefit but also the good of the company. The reasons vary, but some companies, unknowingly or not, see employees as transitory, largely replaceable. Others know they don't know what to do and (correctly) fear the consequences of taking inappropriate action. Whatever the case, a significant portion of all employees have problems severe enough to diminish their effectiveness at work, and without their support, a company will not achieve its goals.

For far too long now we have misunderstood and largely underestimated the interdependency of our personal and work lives, to the detriment of both. The good news is we can fix this.

The First Change Is in Your Mind—You Have to Want It

If you are not committed to doing what is necessary, your desired personal and business change objectives will not happen. Understand that "wanting it" comes with significant strings attached.

Meaningful change can be very difficult to accomplish, so even if you absorb all the suggestions, advice, and techniques related to bringing about positive change, it's not enough. You have still more to do. Here's a personal example.

One of my earliest aspirations was learning to play the guitar. Without realizing it, playing guitar was my goal (i.e., goal in the planning sense). Over the years, I've owned at least a dozen guitars; with one exception, none were particularly expensive. To that investment add the cost of a few lessons and many, many incidentals (strings, cases, straps, picks, how-to books, and assorted whatnots).

Given the number of years and amount of money I've invested in guitar playing, you might reasonably conclude that I must be pretty good by now. Unfortunately, I'm not.

I first decided to take up guitar as a teenager, but I've reached that decision many times since. Oh, I have picked up a few things along the way and can fool some people into thinking I know more than I do. But, frankly, a few minutes of noodling is all I have to show for my time, money, and effort.

What happened? What prevented me from learning to play? Well, I simply didn't practice. Even when taking lessons, I didn't practice often enough over a long enough period of time to achieve my goals. Practice is required for a lot of things many of us like or want to do well, including golf, dance, art, and, yes, playing the guitar. If you don't work at it, you won't achieve your goal. When it came to the guitar, I just didn't do the work.

Contrary to what I've shared throughout this book, I never established a plan that was designed to achieve my goal of learning to play. In fact, I never even thought about the guitar relative to planning. Had I done so, I suspect one of two things would have occurred: (1) I would have correctly identified every step I needed to take, worked my way through those steps becoming a guitar player, or (2) I would have correctly identified everything I needed to do, decided there was no way I would do that, and let go of the desire to play guitar, saving myself a considerable amount of wasted money, time, and frustration in the process.

However, even though I didn't have a plan, I did have a goal (learn to play the guitar), so what prevented me from doing it? Others learn, why not me? We don't have to consider this at length to realize that I thought nothing of the specifics that would be necessary were I to achieve my goal. I had no vision, strategy, tactics, and assessment of what I would need. I had literally nothing more than a desire to play, and as important as that is, it's nowhere near enough to overcome the absence of everything else.

Reflecting on my efforts, I now see that although I wanted to play, I didn't want it badly enough to make the effort to achieve that goal. The act of planning, had I understood and done it early on, would have made that obvious, again, saving me a lot of frustration and some money.

It's no different with anything else in our lives. If you really want something, you have to plan to make it happen. Without defining and following a course of action, adjusting it as needed, the chances of achieving anything significant are greatly diminished. If a goal matters to you or the important people in your life, it deserves planning.

Is the process necessary to achieve a goal such as playing guitar the same or even similar to that of dealing with more serious issues such as substance abuse or a relationship crisis? And regardless of the goal, are there no physical or psychological issues that come into play? If there are, what then?

We all have problems—some worse than others, some biological, some psychological—and we won't always be able to recognize and build into our plans ways to address those problems. For example, addicts are often the last to recognize the severity of their problems. For them, help often comes through the actions of someone else. Quite often, people in trouble can barely function on a day-to-day basis and certainly will not be capable of creating a plan to change behavior they themselves may not recognize as self-destructive. In those cases, recognition of the situation may only come from someone else, and even then that knowledge may not be enough to cause people with the problem to participate in a process leading to change.

There is no simple solution; sometimes bad situations need to get significantly worse (the proverbial rock bottom) before real change is possible. If you see yourself in that last sentence, you have taken the first and most meaningful step to bring about change. You recognize the need. Next, you must begin the process that will lead to the change you wish to make. That may well require assistance from others, including professionals who can help you create a workable plan.

Not learning to play guitar has had little significant bearing on my life, so my lack of planning has only one real consequence: I don't know how to play guitar. But that is vastly different from trying to change a behavior that was preventing me from living life to the fullest.

In short, not all problems are the same, and you must clearly evaluate each change you wish to make so that you can identify and take the right steps as early in the process as possible. And if you realize you cannot do even this much on your own, ask for help.

YES BUT…

Few of us take these first steps as soon as we should, and Dr. Wayne W. Dyer explains why in *Excuses Begone! How to Change Lifelong, Self-Defeating Thinking Habits.*[27] Dr. Dyer has written extensively on several topics I loosely categorize as self-improvement, and, to be honest, my initially narrow-minded reaction was "just another touchy-feely Birkenstock guru talking about contemplating one's inner-self." Still, if I was going to learn how to bring about more positive change, I could not justify ignoring any potentially valuable information he may have to offer. In retrospect, I'm glad I opened my mind to his views because his "no excuses" message is critical to achieving not only personal change but also business change.

Dr. Dyer approaches his subject from the softer side most often found in self-help books. However, he does so in a way that makes an extremely positive contribution, one I now believe is central in importance to anyone wishing to make positive change happen more often.

I strongly recommend *Excuses Begone!*, but until you read that book, consider his core message. Dr. Dyer believes there are many reasons we may not achieve our life's goals, but the biggest obstacles are the ones of our own making. He has identified the following nineteen excuses that prevent us from even attempting change:

1. It will be difficult.
2. It's going to be risky.
3. It will take a long time.
4. There will be family drama.
5. I don't deserve it.
6. It's not my nature.
7. I can't afford it.
8. No one will help me.
9. It has never happened before.
10. I'm not strong enough.
11. I'm not smart enough.
12. I'm too old.

THE 7 KEYS TO CHANGE

13. I'm too young.

14. Rules won't let me.

15. It's too big.

16. I don't have the energy.

17. It's my personal family history, and I can't change that.

18. I'm too busy.

19. I'm too scared.

How many of these sound familiar? Consider the personal and business changes you have attempted and failed to make—or have only considered and abandoned—because you believed one or more of these excuses would prevent success.

You are to be forgiven if you are now reviewing your own list while muttering to yourself, "Yes, but in *my* case, I was (fill in any creative justification you prefer for using one or more of the above excuses)."

We take comfort in believing we have valid explanations for our inability to create change, but what we really have are just excuses. I never learned to play guitar because it would be difficult and take a long time. I now not only recognize my past excuses but also understand why I gave myself permission to use them.

The importance of this cannot be overstated. There are numerous reasons you may never achieve some of your stated personal or business goals, but excuses you give yourself should not be among them.

IN BUSINESS AND PERSONAL

If you are a business manager, you need to be aware of how the mental blocks of your employees will impact the change initiatives you ask them to address. And although your ability to help employees with this in their personal lives is limited, at the very least, you must understand that their ability to function on a professional level, will, to varying degrees, be hampered by their personal problems.

If you are looking at this from the standpoint of your personal life, much the same applies—with one added advantage or disadvantage. The first person you must deal with is yourself. As difficult as it may be, you must critically self-analyze your motives, beliefs, fears, and expectations regarding how much you can accomplish. As you do you must also recognize and eliminate the blocks you have imposed on yourself. As Dr. Dyer might say, "Excuses begone!"

As a manager dealing with company change, or someone attempting personal change, understand that the existence of these blocks will significantly increase the chances of failure. Identifying and defusing them will certainly contribute to success.

KEY #4

What, How, How Much, When, and Who: Planning to Change

I am a business-planning consultant, and positive change is supposedly a by-product of my work. Prior to preparing to write this book, I thought I knew what that process was. I did not, at least not enough to improve the odds of my clients achieving significantly better results than would otherwise happen.

So what about you? And perish the thought if you believe that simply wishing things were different will work. It won't. You must approach desired change with considerable care and planning. Planning is at the center of bringing about business and personal change no matter how few people really understand that point. But as I discovered, there is more to it than that.

In addition to understanding the requirements of planning, you must also understand change management—a related but different discipline. So how do you fill in the gaps in your knowledge?

I began by searching Amazon for titles related to the phrase change management. On the one hand, the results were encouraging because the search generated 12,000+ book titles. On the other hand, there were 12,000+ book titles. No matter how motivated you are to learn, there is no practical way to determine which of those 12,000 are worth your time and money.

Clearly, I needed to do more searching before jumping in and reading (or skimming) however many books I could manage. So in addition to looking for books, I also began searching online for what others were saying about change management, and, not unexpectedly, I found quite a bit.

Descriptions such as "a series of business practices"; "a defined, standardized process"; "company-specific methods"; or simply "a process" were common. With due respect to those who use those terms, all these phrases are true in the same way someone says "a thing" to describe a desk, a car, or a television. They are all things, but that does nothing to help those trying to understand what they are.

As an aside, it shouldn't be a surprise that this happens in business in general and specifically in planning and change management. Business writing is littered with largely meaningless jargon. (If you doubt this, refer to almost any Dilbert cartoon.)

Finally, curiously, some sources link change management exclusively or primarily to information technology or product planning, as if there were no other aspects of business that would benefit from the change management process.

"WHAT ABOUT ME?"

Notice anything missing? None of these examples mention personal change. To be sure, numerous books address changing aspects of one's life, no doubt including some of those 12,000+ change management books. But I never found them.

It's as if change in business is far more worthy of examination and discussion than change in our personal lives. However, at the risk of repeating myself, people who cannot deal with change at home will be equally ineffective in dealing with change at work. So how best to do both? Either the change process in business is not the same for personal issues or they are very similar (or even identical). Before deciding which scenario is more likely, review what has been written about change.

The psychology literature is rich with descriptions of the process of change (some of it contradictory), including the specific stages of change. For example, the German-American psychologist Kurt Lewin said that change takes three forms: (1) unfreeze or releasing those things that bind one to the present, (2) the change itself, and (3) the change, once made, is again frozen.[28]

Possibly the most famous and oft-quoted description of one specific type of change (dealing with grief) came from Elisabeth Kübler-Ross, whose 1969 work titled *On Death and Dying* identified five stages of change: denial, anger, bargaining, depression, and acceptance.[29] In 1975, she developed the more all-inclusive "change curve" with seven stages: shock, denial, frustration, depression, experiments, decisions, and integration. Her focus was not on business, but the change curve can be applied to business with very little adjustment of terminology.

In his 1980 book titled *Managing Transitions: Making the Most of Change*, William Bridges simplified the stages of change, describing just three: ending, neutral, and new beginning.[30]

Also in 1980, Richard Beckhard and David Gleicher went so far as to postulate a formula for determining whether change was even possible (D x V x F > R).[31] Their contention: Only when the product of dissatisfaction with things, the vision of what could be, and the first steps taken to correct things exceeds the resistance to change is change possible.

And to the primarily psychological approach to change, we can add an almost endless list of change theorists who mix elements of psychology with a few nods to business, often influenced by traditional self-help discussions. A good example of this comes from Kris Hallbom, who described seven stages (creation, growth, complexity to maturity, turbulence, chaos, dropping off, and mediation and dormancy) as "the universal cycles of change."[32]

Two books that I found most useful were *The Heart of Change* by John P. Kotter and Dan S. Cohen[33] and *EPIC Change: How to Lead Change in the Global Age* by Timothy R. Clark.[34] Both take a typical business-oriented approach to describing the process of change that mostly tells the reader what must be done rather than how he or she should do it. However, this in no way diminishes the value of what these authors have to say. You cannot worry about *how* you will do something until you first know *what* it is.

With apologies for over simplification, let's consider the key points of both, starting with *The Heart of Change*. Kotter and Cohen describe eight requirements for change:

1. The need to create a sense of urgency
2. The necessity to assemble a guiding team charged with providing change leadership
3. The creation by this team of a clear, sensible vision and strategy to be used to facilitate change
4. Clear and efficient communication of this vision and strategy to all affected
5. The identification and removal of obstacles that could block the process of change
6. The need to incorporate that which will be seen as meaningful, short-term "wins" which, when achieved, will demonstrate the progress necessary to keep the initiative moving forward
7. The need to continually ensure momentum to keep the process moving forward
8. With the desired change completed or largely complete, the need to shift emphasis to making sure that desired behaviors necessary to institutionalize change are in place

With some similarity, Clark builds his case around four stages of change, which are summarized in the acronym EPIC:

Evaluation: During evaluation, the leader continually evaluates competitive reality, internal performance, and alternatives for change as the rest of the organization maintains its current systems.

Preparation: During the preparation stage, the task is to analyze alternative paths for change through experimentation, modeling, testing, and trialing options.

Implementation: During implementation, the organization attempts to achieve the desired results by executing the tasks that were planned during preparation.

Consolidation: When change consolidates, the motivation generated becomes gradually and permanently stronger than the resistance and inertia that opposes it.

Anyone seriously interested in change management should undertake an independent review of the literature available on the subject, in addition to reading the literature on planning. If you do, you will see commonality of thought and areas of agreement, even though in many cases the terms and language are quite different from one author to the next. Often, the differences have to do with the complexity and nuances of the topic, particularly as it pertains to terms (goals versus objectives, vision versus mission, etc.), which are not of great importance. Instead, after you have working knowledge of both planning and change management, your emphasis should shift to the creation of a plan designed to achieve your goals.

So what do these thousands of books and countless articles all addressing change management and planning, both in business and our personal lives, tell us? That could be a completely separate and extremely lengthy book itself; however, for our purposes I summarize the key points as follows.

WHAT

The first requirement is to define not only what you want to change but also, of greater importance, what you want it or you to become. What you call these definitions (goals, objectives, milestones, etc.) is of little importance, but it is essential that you do this step correctly. If you get it wrong, nothing else will matter.

Use positive rather than negative terms to define the results of your desired changes. The distinction between the two is significant. For example, if your strategy calls for business expansion, the appropriate goal might be "to establish operations in Taiwan, Hong Kong, and Seoul prior to midyear" compared with "to cease doing business only in the United States." Likewise, if your personal change initiative has to do with your weight, a more appropriate goal might be "I want to be happy with the way I look" compared with "I don't want to be fat." Express what you want, not what you don't want.

HOW

After you know what you want to change, you can then move to create the plan to achieve those goals. This is just as true in your personal life as it is in business.

After the goals are identified, the next step is to develop an overriding strategy to achieve those goals. In the case of our business example, a strategy might be "to establish strategic partnerships with sales organizations in each location." For our personal goal of being happy, a strategy might be "to get to know individuals who work in areas of interest to me."

With this done, we move to define the tactics we will use in accordance with our strategy. Continuing with the business example, this might include the following: "To conduct an online search of potential sales partners and visit the top three candidates within the first six months of new fiscal year." For our personal goal, this might include the following: "To join a local weekend running club within next two weeks" or "to apply for part-time work at no less than two local running stores within next two weeks."

Notice that when talking about strategy, the description is fairly general and open, whereas tactics are specific, including dates, amounts, and so forth.

HOW MUCH

With strategy and tactics defined, you can focus on the resources and people you will need to execute the plan, much of which will involve cost (hence, how much). What that cost is may or may not be known, and in the case of most significant change initiatives, you will likely be missing things that will be critical to your success. Don't let that discourage you and certainly do not look at these deficiencies as reasons why you cannot plan for the change you wish to see happen. They are simply obstacles to be identified and overcome. Remember, "Excuses begone!"

WHEN

With how much complete, we include key milestone and due dates, both of which are critical details. Getting things done on time or—better still—ahead of schedule, is just as important as doing them. In fact, timeliness is in some ways more important because many actions done late will produce results no better than had they not been done at all.

WHO

Finally, identify who will be responsible for completing the critical tasks that must be done on time and on budget. Accomplishing business and personal change initiatives are a collective effort. Don't imagine you are alone; you only make change happen through the efforts of many.

If you complete these five steps, you will have a plan. You will know *what* you want to happen, *how* you will make it happen, *how much* it will cost, *when* things will be done, and *who* will do what must be done.

(ALMOST) DONE!

The final and in many ways most important requirement is to discipline yourself to not simply follow the plan or—worse yet—ignore it altogether, but to review and change it as often as necessary. Given inevitable changes in circumstances (most everything in the plan is an assumption on day one), you know before you start that changes to your plan will be necessary. That's okay. What you have is a point of departure with a roadmap of where you are headed—a roadmap you can and must adjust as assumptions evolve to reality.

The format you choose to keep track of all this is up to you, and there are many good books on planning that include plan templates, with most of them saying pretty much the same thing:

- What are you going to do? (what)
- How will you do it? (how)
- How much will it cost? (how much)
- When will it be done? (when)
- Who will do it? (who)

The following is one way to keep track of that information. In this case, it provides an example of someone's personal vision to "become a happier, more content person."

YOUR CHART FOR CHANGE

VISION
Become a happier, more content person.

STRATEGY
Reduce personal debt and improve fitness and health.

GOALS

1. Decrease monthly expenditures by $250.

2. Reduce credit card debt to a maximum
   of $3,000 within 6 months.

3. Decrease daily caloric intake to a maximum
   of 2,000 calories.

4. Drop blood pressure to a maximum 120/80.

WHAT	HOW	HOW MUCH	WHEN	WHO	GOAL
Develop and maintain record of all personal expenditures.	Carry notepad and note all charge and cash expenditures. Review after 30 days with goal of eliminating 15% or more.	N/A (not applicable)	Immediately, ongoing	Me	1, 2
Review other family member credit card expenditures looking for minimum 10% monthly reduction.	Discuss with all with credit card access, looking for suggestions to reach 10% reduction target.	N/A	Assemble data within 5 days;; review with family no later than 5 days later.	I will do review and will discuss with each family member with credit card access.	1, 2
Reduce restaurant lunches during week from 5 days to 1 day.	Make lunch for work following dietary guidelines for reducing blood pressure and controlling weight.	Cost of lunch made at home estimated to be $2 daily.	Immediately	Me. Explain to lunch companions asking for their support.	All
Establish minimum monthly credit card payment plan necessary to achieve target reduction.	Meet with bank to determine what minimum monthly payment should be given reduction goal.	Unknown but significant in terms of reduced interest cost.	No later than October 15.	Me, bank employee	1, 2
Begin daily exercise program.	Daily 30 minute walks, increasing to 3 miles daily within 60 days maximum.	N/A immediately; possibly $50 for shoes within the next 60 days.	Start tomorrow; daily thereafter.	Me	3, 4

I can hear it now, "Are you kidding? You expect me to actually write out what I should do?"

I don't. This admittedly very wonkish looking document might be what we use in business but certainly not at home. Life is much too, well, "life," for us to do that. We live in the now and don't have time to write plans to lose fifteen pounds, lower our blood pressure, or balance the household budget. And even if we did, we don't need to. We can certainly identify and do what we must to change the things we want to change.

On the contrary, I don't expect many will do this, but whether you write things down, regardless of whether you take things to the point of having even a mental much less written plan, the specific steps you see in this example are the key elements for whatever change you wish to make. How you define them, keep track of them, and actually do them are up to you.

But if we were to do all of this in our business and personal lives, would we be rewarded in the form of greater success in achieving change initiatives? Not necessarily. Written or otherwise, all of this is absolutely essential, but without the following, success is anything but assured.

YOU CAN'T DO IT ALONE

Nearly every business book addressing change or planning talks about the need for employee buy-in, which is achieved by communicating the urgency of the need for change, followed by getting the right people involved. Without the hard, dedicated work of many, change will not happen.

This is critical, but of greater importance is ensuring that these people, whoever they are, are in the right frame of mind to do what needs to be done. Attempting change with those who are not essential to the process is the one single factor that derails more business change initiatives than anything else.

And what about personal change initiatives? I purposely referenced business change initiatives because that is where the importance of getting help from others is emphasized. Yet read a sample of self-help books and, as the genre implies, the emphasis is definitely on "self," with an overabundance of references to "you." Make no mistake about it, any significant change, business and personal, will happen only as the result of a collective effort.

Earlier, I suggested there were two possible alternatives for creating change: use the same practices for business and personal change or different ones for each. Having considered all that followed, I am convinced there is (fortunately) only one approach to creating positive change. Although, depending on circumstances, what you must do varies in terms, interpretation, and application, the steps for achieving change are the same. Learn them and apply them, and your success bringing about positive change in both business and personal lives will increase significantly.

A final note on the role of human nature in the process of change: Regardless of which methodology you decide to follow, guard against slowing down too much or—worse—stopping altogether, particularly during periods of radical change. By itself, human inertia is enough to derail a change effort.

If you cannot overcome the natural tendency toward the status quo, things will change without your direction, perhaps in a way you may not like. All the understanding you may have about what to do aside, if you are not willing to start and keep going, you will not get where you want to be.

Change Success Traps: Common Mistakes You Don't Need to Make

Let's start with you.

Much of what has been written regarding the process of change, including how to make change initiatives more successful, has understated the importance of the individual—you.

True, most every book and article addressing business change will, at some point, talk about the need for buy-in, telling management they must get employees to not only accept the need for change but also enthusiastically support it. But this is what not how, with the dismal results previously discussed suggesting something is still very wrong.

However, before you agree, thinking how little attention your boss gives you, consider what you have done to better prepare to make positive change happen, both in business and your personal life.

Chances are…not enough.

The existence of an enormous amount of published content regarding change management does not guarantee that those who need the information will ever read it. And if they are reading it, they may not be practicing what they've learned.

A third possibility is that mistakes are made when attempting to plan or implement change. Let's examine some of those mistakes so that you can avoid them.

Inherent in every major change initiative, business and personal, should be a plan, and at the core of every plan are several elements that must be present and correct. This usually includes a vision of what is to happen; possibly a mission statement; certainly goals, which may or may not also include objectives; a plan strategy; and finally specific tactics, which, when executed properly, will hopefully lead to achievement of the goals.

If you recite this list to almost any mid- to senior-level manager (especially those with MBAs), you'll see heads nodding. So there's little reason to dwell on the minutia of plan elements, right? Experience suggests otherwise.

To begin, the differences among some of these terms—notably, goals and objectives, vision and mission, and sometimes even strategy and tactics—spark significant—sometimes loud—discussion. For proof, simply search online for the following terms: "the difference between goals and objectives" and "the difference between vision and strategy." You will find more than you likely expect.

Me? I use whatever labels make the planning team I'm working with most comfortable, staying out of the ongoing terminology fray. You can do the same by using only those terms that make the most sense to you. Whether you are part of a management team in a company or an individual, focus on what you want to do (your vision, goals, and objectives) as well as how you will make this happen (the strategy you will use followed by the specific tactics or things you will do).

The second area where management teams and individuals come off the path has to do with confusing goals and tactics. Consider the following example:

Company A's management set a goal of a 15 percent increase in sales, planning to go from $100 million to $115 million in annual revenue. To do this, it will focus on increasing sales, doing things that might result in extra cost, such as higher marketing expenditures, additional expense for opening new territories, increased head count in sales, and the cost of more aggressive sales programs. The reality is that following this plan may result in company A achieving its sales target while sacrificing profits in the short term.

In many instances, this is anticipated and presents no problem, but in this case there's a twist. Company A's ownership intends to sell the business based on a high multiple of pretax profit, and any activity that lowers profit will be at odds with its goal of selling. How is this conflict resolved?

To begin, the owner's primary mistake was not telling management about the intent (goal) to sell. Had they done so, management could have focused on formulating goals in line with the expectations of its stockholders. For example, the goal might have been to increase pretax profit by X percent or $X compared with increasing sales. A sales increase could still be a part of the plan—as a tactic ("increase sales 10 percent") in support of a corporate goal of expansion ("establish three new territories within the first six months of the new calendar year").

Confusing goals with tactics is not limited to business. My unhappily married friend, described in an earlier chapter, viewed divorce as an end-goal just as many financially pressed families today are looking at bankruptcy as a positive solution to their money problems. Although both could be the hoped-for deliverance, they will more likely lead to completely different outcomes than those expected or desired.

Finally, assuming we do not let terminology and definitions get in the way of our personal and business change initiatives, what's left to derail our efforts?

It bears repeating: No significant change, personal or business, is ever accomplished by a single individual. Real change happens through the concerted efforts of a few to many individuals all working toward a common goal. This is a given in business, where companies establish change teams with complete understanding that anything worth doing will require the efforts of many. However, when it comes to our personal lives, how many of us have ever assembled a change team?

So how do you decide whom you need to recruit to help you bring about change? Let's begin by first considering what often happens in business.

ABILITY, NOT RANK

At many companies, the president or the CEO develops the change vision and then assembles a change team consisting of his or her direct reports, often division or functional vice presidents or directors. The reason for change will be explained, the vision will be articulated, and the change team will then begin its work to make it happen.

The problem is that often little or no consideration is given to how appropriate these individuals are for the tasks ahead. They are put on the team based on rank, position, or title, along with an expectation of their ability to perform. The CEO fails to consider their mind-sets, assuming that members of senior management will know what to do, and they'll be able to do it as part of the team. Unfortunately, the reality is often quite different.

The correct approach is to recruit individuals with the mind-set, skills, and training necessary to increase the chances for success. Although this may include senior management, perhaps it doesn't. The better choice may be to recruit less senior employees, possibly even nonmanagement, whose perspective is not limited to the status quo. However, keep in mind that although this solves one problem, it might create another: the resistance of senior managers not selected for the change team. But that said, assembling the most effective team is paramount, and management will have to deal with the important but secondary issue of the reaction of those not selected.

MEET HAL, A TEAM PLAYER

One of the survey calls I received came from Hal, who wanted to talk about his desire to change the direction of his career. It soon became clear that he had been in a position where misidentification of a change team had created an enormous problem, for not only him but also his company.

Hal was in his late fifties, perhaps five years from retirement, when his company CEO called for a major strategic shift. As a vice president and an executive committee member, Hal and three of his peers were tasked with fleshing out the CEO's vision, including drafting a tactical plan. The other vice presidents were also in their fifties, and none were particularly interested in taking a lot of risk. They all felt that what they had been doing was working and should not be disturbed.

Even so, Hal said he and the others were good corporate soldiers who would do their best to meet the CEO's expectations. After all, loyalty and willingness to tow the company line helped them achieve their current positions.

They began meeting to devise a strategy that would be followed by the development of a tactical plan. However, the CEO rejected every promising possibility they suggested. "At first, we began to question ourselves; were we really up to the task?" Hal said. "But after one too many meetings with little or nothing to show for our efforts, we no longer felt we were the problem. Instead, we concluded the CEO really didn't know what he wanted, and nothing we said was going to change that."

Finally, the team decided to confront the CEO with the problem they believed he had created. During the next review meeting, rather than presenting yet another strategy, they told him they had no idea what he wanted. They welcomed his input but were simply out of ideas given his rejection of everything they had come up with to that point.

I asked Hal about the company's business and the CEO's vision. He said they did contract printing of proprietary company magazines, an industry in decline as more and more publications were published in digital form. The CEO's vision, as best Hal could explain it, had to do with moving from analog printing to creating and hosting of online client publications. Hal said it sounded like the CEO "wanted us old print guys to turn into Internet gurus, and none of us knew how or wanted to do that."

Many more meetings followed as the CEO attempted to lead his team in the development of a strategy and tactical plan to transform the company. As time passed, they all came to the realization that they could not develop and execute the new vision with the current leadership.

Hal felt he and his peers did what they could to fill the gaps in their knowledge, but he said the CEO "wasn't tolerant of our efforts, and, in the end, I decided it was time for me to go." He negotiated a twelve-month termination salary as part of his early retirement and left after twenty-seven years with the company.

YOU'RE IN CHARGE OF YOU

You are the "CEO" of your life, and it's up to you to lay the foundation for the changes you wish to make. This includes identifying the vision of what you want to achieve, which is followed by defining the goals that will represent the achievement of that vision. With that done, you move on to identify the resources you will need to achieve your goals. Here, again, a word of caution is in order. Don't fool yourself by thinking you can do it all; you can't. Just as in business, you will need help from others with knowledge, talent, and expertise you don't have.

Having reached a decision to attempt meaningful change, including recognizing that the help of others will be necessary, many people look to close friends and family members. But no matter how willing and well intentioned they may be, they are not always the best choices. Indeed, they could be at the center of the problem. Instead, widen your search to others, including those you may not know very well, if at all, as well as those whose services will cost money. (Don't ask an amateur to do a professional's job. You often won't get what you don't pay for.)

In the course of researching this book, I was fortunate to talk with several people about their personal change initiatives, and one thing became very clear very quickly. Asking for help outside one's circle of friends and family is a foreign concept, particularly when the issues are extremely personal. Get over it! You will need help, and the sooner you identify those who can provide it, the better off you will be.

But unfortunately not everyone sees this, including Hal, who ended up with a year's salary and soon after, lots of free time.

HAL 2.0

After the stress of the CEO's demands was gone, Hal said he was re-energized and finally in a position to pursue his own vision of a new company. He would not only replace his lost income but would also do something he would enjoy as part of his retirement.

Although he understood that electronic publishing had reduced the need for print, Hal was convinced that many small businesses could benefit from having in-house print publications. With that in mind, he founded his own company to act as a broker/consultant to create publications, advising small businesses about their use for marketing. He made a modest investment in a new computer, business cards, stationary, a company brochure, and set to work.

Six months in, with just six months left on his early retirement payout, Hal had not landed a single client. He gave up his dream and began looking for any position that would the pay the bills after he received the last check from his former employer. He soon found work as a commissioned salesperson for a printing company; a position similar to one he had at the beginning of his career—with a commensurately smaller salary. His wife had kept her job, and although they had assumed they would retire in their early sixties, that was no longer feasible.

What went wrong? Did Hal experience a classic case of "entrepreneurial blindness," offering a product or a service no one wants?

PLANNING TO FAIL

When a new venture fails, it's a good idea to spend at least some time looking for the reasons. Perhaps the pricing was wrong or the distribution strategy was not in keeping with how the product should be offered to customers. Perhaps the idea was good, but progress wasn't happening quickly enough to generate sufficient income. In Hal's case, however, none of this was true; the reason his new business failed was painfully obvious; Hal had absolutely no plan for success.

He later admitted the idea of owning a business was something he had considered only occasionally. When he left his old job, he did little more than print some business cards and begin to call on what he felt were potential customers. With not so much as the legal formalities for his new company determined (Hal said there was no point in doing that until he knew for certain he had a viable business), and certainly no thought about vision, strategy, or tactics, he began operation. In other words, Hal acted no differently than I had when I decided I wanted to play guitar.

As if launching a business with absolutely no plan isn't bad enough, Hal compounded his problems by not seeking help or advice from anyone other than his wife. In that regard, his error was similar to that committed by his former CEO (asking the wrong people to develop a plan). His wife was a teacher, and as capable an educator as she might be, she was not the right person to advise him on his business venture.

The debate about whether getting the wrong help with a major change initiative is a bigger mistake than getting no help aside, Hal managed to do both.

If bringing about major change in our lives were easy, more people would be doing so more successfully. Why further reduce your chances for success by picking the wrong people to help you or by attempting to go it alone? Too much evidence suggests that neither scenario will work.

KEY #6

Change Timing:
Evolution or Revolution

No meaningful change happens quickly and even I was surprised to see how much time is necessary to accomplish the more ambitious goals in our personal and business lives. For example, most of those writing about how to create major change in large corporate organizations say progress is not measured in weeks or months but in years. Unfortunately, in a world where stockholders demand quarterly returns on investment, we don't give management years to deliver results. However, that aside, the need for time to make change happen is reality nevertheless.

Likewise, as individuals, we want quick fix solutions for almost everything. If we want to lose twenty-five pounds, we look for a diet that will shed the weight in days not weeks, health be damned. But wanting something is not the same as getting it, so be prepared to not only work at it but to wait for it as well. Like our grandmothers said, "All things in due time"—a lesson it took me some time to learn (no pun intended).

THE GRANDMA PRINCIPLE

Until my mid-thirties, my career had consisted of working in larger companies, usually as the head of sales and marketing. The exception to this was a start-up that recruited me. Thinking about the offer, I had visions of entrepreneurial freedom along with what I assumed would be very lucrative founders stock. All we needed to do was complete a secondary round of venture capital financing, a goal I was told would be achieved within six months of my start date.

We did find the investment capital but not in six months. It was more like three years later. During that time, we adopted every conceivable expense containment tactic imaginable, including accepting additional common stock in lieu of salary—all designed to conserve dwindling cash reserves. But when the money came, so did an investor-mandated new CEO who soon concluded that my marketing and sales skills were redundant to his. So, at thirty-five years of age, I was again pondering my next move.

In reality, I had felt the pull to be on my own much earlier and had, in my off time, been planning an entrepreneurial venture I would one day launch. So when free to find my next career, my reaction was a hybrid of excitement and fear. I could now execute the plan I had worked so hard to create! But how would I provide for my wife and toddler—whose little brother was due to be born in a few months? Sometimes opportunity is thrust on us. Ready or not, mine had arrived.

Based on my previous three years at a start-up company, I should have clearly understood the value of overestimating the time necessary to accomplish things. I had seen numerous missed due dates resulting from underestimating how long meaningful change can take. I should have understood this and probably could have, but I didn't.

Instead, I was infected with an entrepreneurial malaise that causes its victims to overvalue their own thinking. I incorrectly planned for profitable operations and a sustainable income within six months, an estimate that proved wrong by approximately two and a half years. Fortunately, the company I founded, much evolved and changed from my original vision, became a success and was ultimately purchased by a larger concern under terms incredibly favorable to me. But things could have easily gone the other way, if for no other reason than my underestimating how long survival would take prior to experiencing real success.

GRANDMA WAS RIGHT

Regardless of whether you are charged with bringing about change in business or simply want to fix things in your personal life, take the time necessary to ensure that you identify the right vision, the right goals, the right strategy, the right tactics, and the right people to help—all before you begin the change effort. Anything less will likely end in failure and—worse—make it that much more difficult when you attempt to bring about other changes in the future.

Meaningful change takes time, and although there are some overnight successes, don't count on being one of them. We are talking about your life, and nothing less than the time necessary to accomplish your goals is what you will need to do what you want to do.

TIME TO CHANGE?

What will happen and when it will happen vary greatly with each circumstance. Some change occurs at a relatively fixed rate, whereas the timing for other change varies considerably. Is the change you face (or want to face) evolutionary, proceeding at a relatively slow pace, or revolutionary, unfolding at a speed that makes it difficult to keep up? Your ability to manage what happens next hinges on your answer.

To better understand the importance of change timing, consider a river that will, in time, overflow its banks as a result of excessive rain. In many cases, the resulting increase in water volume is somewhat predictable. Those living near the river know that if the water continues to rise at a steady, predictable rate, they will most likely have time to protect their property or evacuate if necessary. Although it might be a stretch to say the steadily rising river is undergoing evolutionary change, it does so relative to a sudden, unexpected increase. In that case, flash flooding would be a revolutionary change in the river.

You can, no doubt, imagine many examples of evolutionary versus revolutionary rates of change. No one has ever gotten a cavity overnight. The change to the tooth occurs over time.

Anyone who has broken a bone understands the concept of a revolutionary change in health. One minute you're fine, and the next minute you're in tremendous pain, heading to the nearest emergency room. Your priorities and perspective have changed quickly!

Obviously, no one spends hours pondering the optimal timing for the treatment of cavities or broken bones. We know from experience how much time is required. But what about situations where this is not as clear? Let's look at business, political, and personal examples, concentrating on the timing for each.

BUSINESS

In 1980, General Motors, Ford, and Chrysler dominated the American automobile industry. The combined U.S. market share of the so-called Big Three was approximately 75 percent, with the balance of the market split among all other manufacturers. By 2010, the Big Three's market share had dropped to 40 percent, depending on which segments of the market were included.[35] In other words, the U.S. new vehicle manufacturers' market share was cut in half in thirty years. Was this evolutionary or revolutionary change timing?

Much has since been written regarding what the management of those three companies were thinking as foreign manufacturers, particularly the Japanese, boosted their market share year after year. At the very least GM, Ford, and Chrysler grossly underestimated the potential threat of foreign brands, both from a product and timing perspective.

Although the major U.S. car manufacturers have since stabilized their market positions and are now turning out what most consider to be world-class vehicles, a return to their 1980s-era dominance is unlikely. Indeed, the Big Three is now the Big Two since Italian manufacturer Fiat increased its ownership stake in Chrysler to 51 percent. Today, the combined market share of GM and Ford is no more than 30 percent and possibly as low as 25 percent.

That's tremendous change in three decades but is it evolutionary or revolutionary? Looking back, we may well say the former, but if you were an executive at GM, Ford, or Chrysler back in 1980….

Another well-known example of fast-moving change occurred in photography, and no company was more affected than Eastman Kodak.

Kodak, long the leader in photography film and a major player in cameras, was slow to react to the emergence of digital photography. Still, it did introduce what was considered a strong product lineup, and in 2000 it vowed to become the leader in digital camera sales.

Although many business analysts had their doubts about Kodak's viability, by 2005 Kodak ranked number one in U.S. digital camera sales. Kodak's total sales of digital products increased 40 percent to $5.7 billion, whereas sales related to film-based products declined 18 percent in the same period.[36] These statistics appear to vindicate Kodak's stated goal from 2000 and prove that Kodak reacted quickly enough, regardless of whether the industry was undergoing evolutionary or revolutionary change.

However, there is more to the story. In early 2011, Kodak said it was expecting operational earnings moving from minus $200 million to at best break even, on total company revenue between $6.4 billion and $6.7 billion. Its expected 2011 GAAP (generally accepted accounting principles) loss from continuing operations would be in the range of $100 million to as much as $300 million.[37]

In late March 2011, news source Bloomberg reported that Eastman Kodak had won the latest round in a patent dispute with Apple Inc. and Research in Motion Ltd (RIM). This court victory had a potential value worth more than $1 billion in new licensing revenue for the camera company.[38] Finally, in late January 2012, Kodak filed for bankruptcy.

It is unknown at this time if the court judgment will withstand expected challenges from both Apple and RIM or if the protection offered by bankruptcy will be sufficient to keep Kodak from disappearing altogether. In either case, this example shows how a company's fortunes are dependent on not only one or two things but also numerous factors occurring concurrently, each with different timing.

POLITICS

In the last two years, many Middle East governments have come under siege, with their citizens demanding change. The governments of Tunisia, Egypt, and Libya have fallen, the first two within a month of the initial insurrections. Protests continue in Yemen and Syria, and significant change seems a near certainty in those countries as well. Whether it takes weeks, months, or even years, a process of change is underway with much that remains uncertain, not the least of which is timing.

As an elementary school student in the 1950s, I studied the 1940s governments of Japan and Germany, with hindsight, recognizing them as dictatorships destined to go the way of all dictatorships in relatively short order.

In sharp contrast was the Soviet Union (USSR). Although too young to be cognizant of the details of the East/West tensions in the 1950s, I quickly became generally aware of the USSR from what I learned in school and what I saw in newspapers.

Before long, for me the USSR became as much a constant reality as was the United States. I assumed the USSR would endure. Yet seemingly overnight, it disbanded, leaving 15 independent countries in its place.

Is this revolutionary or evolutionary change?

I viewed the demise of the USSR as revolutionary; one day it was there, the next day it was not. I felt this way even though I understood that the challenges the USSR faced might ultimately lead to its dissolution.

However, intellectual perspective and emotional perspective are two very different things. My view of possible changes to the USSR was running on two different change "clocks." My rational mind saw and immediately understood the headlines telling me the USSR was no more, although my emotional mind took much longer to process what that meant. And no doubt anyone my age who lived in a former Soviet republic during this period would certainly perceive events much differently than I did.

PERSONAL

The timing of change in personal matters varies as much as it does in business and politics, with each individual perceiving the changes in his or her life differently from others.

Consider the 50 percent divorce rate discussed earlier. The average length of a marriage that ends in divorce in the United States is eight years[39]—an eternity if problems begin early. However, if couples acknowledge their issues promptly and take action accordingly, divorce might be avoided, and for them, the passage of time would feel much different. The longer problems go unrecognized and addressed, the less likely a marriage can be salvaged.

It all comes down to this: The time required to rectify problems has everything to do with how significant a change is being contemplated. In a troubled marriage, the more severe the problem and the longer it has existed without effort to resolve it, the less likely it is to be resolved.

What about the timing necessary for other change initiatives, such as weight loss? Consider two individuals who each need to lose 10 percent of their current weight. You might assume each would face the same time continuum. However, although numbers do not necessarily lie, they don't always tell the complete truth.

Someone who just recently became 10 percent over his or her ideal weight will view the weight loss goal very differently from someone who has been 10 percent over his or her ideal weight for the last decade. This is true for several reasons, including the ingrained attitudes and habits that make losing excess weight more difficult the longer it has existed.

Weight loss is an industry. A seemingly endless array of books, drugs, supplements, and other products promise to help us lose weight; yet very few do. Why? What the weight loss gurus don't mention is the many other variables that contribute to success or failure.

Even if you pick the right weight loss regimen, if you misjudge the amount of time necessary for you (compared with someone else) to reach your goal weight, you can fail. Frustration with a lack of progress has ended the diets of many.

But when you establish a weight change trigger, understanding that the time necessary for you and a friend to lose the same amount of weight will likely be different, you are ahead of the game. This understanding eliminates one frustrating reality that could derail your efforts: timing.

Finally, consider one of the more time-centric activities faced by all students: the time required to study for a final exam. I recall my parents and some teachers telling me I simply had not studied enough when my test grades were, shall we say, less than optimum. It's not that I felt I had studied sufficiently in every case; I often knew I hadn't. But sometimes when I felt I had studied more than should have been necessary, the results still indicated otherwise.

How much studying was enough? The answer had less to do with what I had to learn and more to do with how much I already knew. A B student preparing for a final exam worth 50 percent of the class grade has significantly less to learn than does a D student studying for the same test, and comparisons of the timelines necessary for each are close to meaningless.

BUY LOW, SELL HIGH!—RIGHT!

As anyone who has ever lost money in the stock market knows, timing is everything. We are just emerging from the worst recession since the 1930s Great Depression, which has caused many Americans to say, "That's it, I'm never investing in the stock market again!"

Yet many who felt that way just one or two years ago are now considering reentering the market given the lack of investment opportunities elsewhere. Good luck in determining whether we are at, near, or are still on our way to the economic bottom. And related to this, good luck determining the timing for recovery in so many industries directly or indirectly related to the stock market. Whatever the correct timing is for all of that is well beyond me and probably most of you as well.

Nevertheless, as difficult as it is to understand investment timing, you cannot ignore it. More than what you invest in, when you invest will likely have more to do with your profit or loss than will anything else.

If all this has you assuming there is no point worrying about timing because there is very little you can do about it, you have reached the wrong conclusion. Change timing is extremely complex, but that in no way diminishes the need to consider its impact on what you wish to do. Although you cannot predict change timing with great accuracy, you can and should make assumptions about what it will be, altering them and your plans as new reality comes to light.

Whether change timing is evolutionary or revolutionary largely depends on the viewpoint of the person considering the timing. There is no actual clock—only our perception of time passing, which, as Einstein proved, is relative to where and how we observe the events being measured.

Is change timing revolutionary or evolutionary? It is.

The Importance
of Attitude

Unlike many books targeting businesspeople, *The 7 Keys to Change* focuses on the specifics of what you need to do to make change happen in business and your personal life.

So what's the *most important* key to making change happen? Your mindset—more so than everything else. The primary roadblock to positive change, the one thing that prevents most people from accomplishing their business and personal goals, is attitude.

Let me be clear: If you don't manage your mind when attempting to manage significant change, you will fail.

To realize your goals, you must direct and control many things, including other people, all with the sole purpose of achieving the desired results. That being said, can there be any doubt about the importance of you controlling you? Is anyone other than you in a better position to make or break your change initiative?

So what do I mean by attitude? What I don't mean is the "good attitude" or "bad attitude" labels that often come to mind when someone hears that word. It helps if your mental state is more positive than negative, but being in a good mood is not enough. You need to be receptive to your own beliefs and goals. You need to believe that you are doing not only all you can but also what you should to produce change. That will be impossible without the right attitude.

In a previous chapter, you read Dr. Wayne Dyer's nineteen excuses for not attempting change. He made it clear that we might as well not bother to attempt change if the first thing we do is give ourselves excuses for why we won't succeed. That makes sense; so all we need to do is deny ourselves those safe haven excuses, put our plan together, manage it, and we're on our way to success. Right? Not quite!

But if you feel that no one will help you (excuse #8), or it will take too long (excuse #3), or you aren't smart enough (excuse #11), how do you change your mind? Make no mistake; you will need to adjust your attitude. If you can't change your mind, how can you expect to change anything else?

I almost missed this last and very important element of the process of change until fate dealt me a lesson in priorities. In fall 2010, I had completed the first draft of this book and was, in my mind, in the editing phase. Thanksgiving was coming up, and I was feeling good about the book, business, and life in general—until "that day."

I went in for a routine checkup, and while my doctor and I chatted, he thumbed through my medical file, stopping when he came to the results of a blood test I had taken a few months earlier. To my surprise, he said the results might indicate a serious medical condition, one that could require surgery, ongoing treatment, and monitoring. Instantly, all thoughts of the holidays, clients, and this book immediately left my mind. I was laser focused on what he had said, even though there were far more assumptions and questions than facts and answers.

If you've faced a medical crisis, you can likely relate to what was going through my mind. I subjugated everything that had only moments before been front and center in my thoughts. I was focused on the threat to my health.

I pride myself on not being the type to panic, and often the best I have to offer emerges when facing a challenge. However, I don't mind admitting I had one hell of a time not panicking. No matter how often my doctor told me to relax while waiting for further test results, hearing that advice and taking that advice were two very different things.

The truth is that I knew what to do and, more important, what not to do. Had this happened to a friend, I would have offered calm, logical counsel, such as "Relax and wait for the diagnosis. You'll be fine." Or "That's treatable. You'll get through this." But as the patient, I was in no mood to hear my own assurances.

In the days that followed, thoughts of negative outcomes came frequently. Dread niggled at the back of my mind. These thoughts were a bit easier to deal with when they moved to the forefront because I was able to use logic to reassure myself. But even on those infrequent occasions when I was able to put my looming diagnosis out of my mind, it would suddenly reappear. And during the worst of times, I was forced to stop everything to ponder what I saw as the most likely outcome.

This was no way to live, especially for someone writing a book telling others how to handle change. Still, my plan was to move forward at a much reduced pace given the newly arrived "elephant" in my mind's "room" that now demanded my attention.

A REALITY CHECK FROM AN OLD FRIEND

About a month into the diagnostic process, I received an e-mail from Anne, a longtime friend I had worked with early in our careers. We stayed in touch through e-mail and occasional dinners she arranged for a group of former colleagues. Anne was simply checking in to see how things were going with my book and life and had no idea about my health concerns. And I had no desire to tell her or anyone else. I was, I told myself, going to deal with this on my own.

I let Anne know the book was going well although slowly due to the holidays and other commitments. I described it as mostly done, in editing, and that I would get back to it in earnest in the New Year. What I didn't say is that I knew one of two things would happen. The tests would reveal a problem requiring surgery and treatment or nothing amiss. The second scenario would mean returning to normal life, finishing the book, but the first….

Responding with her trademark optimism, Anne wrote that she knew the book would be completed and would be well worth reading for everyone who picked it up, including her. She concluded by predicting I would "hit it out of the park as I have known you to do everything in your life."

If this e-mail had come from most anyone else I might have chalked it up to unnecessary hyperbole, but I knew Anne was as sincere now as she'd been in all the years I had known her. Reading her message made me think about her story, which ultimately lead me to conclusions that are very important when attempting to understand what you must do to bring about positive changes in your life.

Let me tell you about Anne so you can understand as I do the importance of the unsaid message in her e-mail.

We met years ago when she joined the marketing and product development department I was in charge of early in my career. We had little direct contact early on because she worked for someone who reported to someone who reported to me. One of my first detailed recollections of her came when she was suddenly hospitalized in her early twenties. One day she became ill and was soon in the hospital undergoing tests that ultimately revealed a life-threatening medical problem.

I can still recall visiting her in the hospital and thinking that she seemed the same as always. She was smiling, joking with visitors, assuring us she would soon be back to work. However, whether she knew it or not, her life had changed dramatically.

Like most twenty-somethings, Anne enjoyed staying out late with friends, occasional social drinking, and more or less carefree eating. Now, everything about her lifestyle had to change. From that moment on she had to carefully monitor her diet and get sufficient sleep. And soon after being released from the hospital, she was back at work, showing little sign of the transformation she was forced to make.

Handling a major health problem in such a positive way is reason enough to admire Anne, but there's more. Soon after her medical condition emerged, she became the target of a stalker—a stranger who to this day, more than twenty-five years later, occasionally attempts to disrupt her life with threats and actions that would ruin the life of many. However, Anne not only handled what life threw at her but also chose to do so with a tremendously positive attitude.

Anne's journey was on my mind when I reread her e-mail. It forced me to quickly realize how I had blown my health situation out of proportion. Whatever I was facing paled in comparison to how she had lived more than half her life. Anne's message (and her life) made me realize that work on this book had slowed because I had allowed it to. And more than just not completing the book, I had put the brakes on life. But the silver lining in that otherwise dark period was my realization that I needed to cover one more topic, something that would equal or exceed in importance everything else I had written.

ATTITUDE!

How do you change or control your attitude, particularly when much of what you are thinking is coming from your subconscious and is seemingly out of your control?

When I first started thinking about why my clients were not doing better than they had, I assumed I only needed to read a few more books on planning to improve the way I approached consulting assignments. However, I found there was much more to it than that. And when I determined that attitude was a key element of the change process, I set out to find authors who might help me not only understand the role attitude plays in the process of change but also, of greater importance, how someone can improve his or her attitude.

I found many books about attitude, changing attitude, positive attitude, and so forth. Numbers aside, the amount of meaningful information I found in the books I reviewed was much less than I found researching planning and change management. Many use a coaching "you can do it" tone that's almost religious in nature. However, "you can do it!" didn't tell me *how* to do it.

Fortunately a few books stood out, including *The Difference Maker: Making Your Attitude Your Greatest Asset* by John C. Maxwell. I have selected some points from his book that help put the importance of attitude into perspective.

To begin, Maxwell does what probably should be obvious and starts by defining attitude. He said, "I think of attitude as an inward feeling expressed by outward behavior."[40]

To paraphrase, attitude is manifested in what we do and say as a result of what we think and feel. As much as I wanted to hide my concern for my health from others, my worry came out in my behavior. Many of my activities were curtailed or abandoned as my focus shifted to my health. The change in my behavior was apparent had I only been looking.

Maxwell also encourages readers to acknowledge that being positive is easy when everything is going well. "Your attitude really only becomes the difference maker when difficult challenges rise before you. In those moments, your attitude is sometimes the only difference between whether you press on or quit."[41]

I couldn't agree more. My life was rolling along just fine, and although I wasn't arrogant about my situation, I did feel that things were going well because of my own abilities. But when a roadblock occurred, I effectively shut down. I didn't even have an official diagnosis, but the very threat of a serious health problem curtailed normalcy. What stopped me was me.

Maxwell warns us of the challenges we will face. "But there are especially difficult hurdles that everyone must overcome in the course of life. I call them the big five attitude obstacles: discouragement, change, problems, fear and failure."[42]

In my opinion, this list errs only in that it includes change as an obstacle. Having studied the subject, I understand why he calls it that; many do inherently fear change. However, the reason we do is because of the other things on his list, all of which are interrelated. Were we better at dealing with discouragement, problems, fear, and failure, we would have greater success in dealing with change.

In my situation, nothing loomed larger than fear. If you envision an undulating wave with peaks and valleys of varying heights and depths, that was my mental state, sometimes changing within minutes, sometimes controlled by me, although certainly in the beginning not nearly as much as I would have liked. I feared change in the sense that my health might change, and, as a result, my life along with it. But much more than that, I feared the consequences of that happening.

But here's the interesting part. I was writing a book about the process of change and how, as much as possible, one must be in charge of everything necessary to bring about positive change. I really believed this, yet the moment I was confronted with a personal obstacle, I failed to sufficiently see the role my own attitude would play in this crisis. In other words, I was standing right in the middle of my own personal "forest" not seeing a single "tree."

Perhaps that overstates it a bit because with all due respect to Maxwell, I really didn't need him or anyone to tell me that was happening. I knew I was fighting a battle with myself and was unable to talk myself "off the ledge."

Maxwell did help me off that ledge when he wrote "Fear and anxiety are debilitating emotions. They are interest paid in advance on the debt you may never owe."[43]

How true is that? I had managed to put myself far down a road I might never be on, seeing outcomes I may never experience. That wouldn't have been so bad assuming I spent equal time envisioning equally positive outcomes. But instead I paid emotional "interest" in advance of incurring the "debt."

Maxwell's book offers much good advice concerning how to deal with a problem that is universal to most all of us, including a quote by the British doctor and preacher D. Martyn Lloyd-Jones, who said in his book *Spiritual Depression: Its Cause and Cure*, "Most of your unhappiness in life is due to the fact that you are listening to yourself rather than talking to yourself."[44]

Think about what that means because it is very important—and true, as my situation proved.

After I knew I might have a problem, my emotions largely took over, ranging from "everything will be okay" to "I'm screwed," with too much emphasis on the latter and not enough on the former. It was only when I forced my intellect to overrule my emotions that I was able to put things in perspective. Only then could I begin to make progress, albeit at a slower pace than I would have liked. Still, I congratulate myself for making any progress at all during that time because part of me wanted to crawl into bed and stay there until somebody swooped in to make everything better.

When I was having negative thoughts, I was doing exactly what Lloyd-Jones describes; in my case, listening to myself, hearing doomsday chatter from God knows where.

What I ultimately did was to stop listening to anything that had little basis in truth. I consciously forced myself to acknowledge the facts, and every time I did, absolutely every time, I reached the right conclusion. Yes, I may have a problem, but it wasn't one without a solution and certainly not one that would end as badly as I had imagined.

If that rationale had emerged on its own, I would have avoided a lot of discomfort, finishing this book much sooner. I could have readily "listened to myself" with little or no need to "talk to myself." However, because that wasn't the case, it was up to me to direct the process.

Maxwell's book is primarily about adapting a positive attitude, and I don't know if he thought his work would have any effect on the change process. Nonetheless, he did say something that ties directly to the purpose of *The 7 Keys to Change*, which helps make the final connection among planning, change management, and the importance of personal attitude: "To change your life, you must make a choice to take responsibility for your attitude, and to do everything you can to make it work for you."[45] Herein is the starting point for all change initiatives: *You must make a choice to take responsibility for your attitude.*

Another valuable book is *Success Through a Positive Mental Attitude* by Napoleon Hill and W. Clement Stone.[46] Published in 1960, it has been revised and is still in print. (Napoleon Hill wrote the classic self-help book *Think and Grow Rich* in 1937. It, too, is still in print.)

As Stone tells it, he became a disciple of Napoleon Hill after reading *Think and Grow Rich* as a young man and attributed his success to what he learned from that book. Stone became a multimillionaire and advisor to presidents until his death in 2002, being 100 years old.

Keeping in mind that Stone's business career largely occurred more than half a century ago, it is testimony to his thinking that much of what he recommended is still valid today. As a planning consultant, I particularly agree with one of his main contentions having to do with identifying goals and objectives that are really what you want to achieve: "98 out of every 100 persons who are dissatisfied with their world do not have a clear picture in their minds of the world they would like for themselves."[47]

More to the point, many people don't know what they want, and in hand with Stone's statement is the old planning truism, "If you don't know where you're going, any plan will get you there."

Along with Maxwell's book, I also see direct connection in Stone's comments to Dr. Dyer's book—in this case, the recognition of the universality of personal problems: "Everyone has problems. This is because you and everything in the universe are in a constant process of change. Change is an inexorable natural law. What is important to you is that your success or failure to meet the challenges of change are dependent upon your mental attitude."[48]

This means we no longer need to worry about having problems because it is a given that we will. And after we acknowledge this, we are then free to devote all our time and resources to solving them—an outcome I find as worth striving to achieve as it is difficult to do.

If having a good attitude is the best, most logical course to take, why not just do it? The problem is how to do it, and Stone offers advice about what he calls "mental vision":

The person who is mentally nearsighted is apt to overlook objects and possibilities that are distant. He pays attention only to the problems immediately at hand and is blind to the opportunities that could be his by thinking and planning in terms of the future. You are nearsighted if you do not make plans, form objectives, and lay the foundation for the future.

On the other hand, the mentally farsighted person is apt to overlook possibilities that are right before him. He does not see the opportunities at hand. He sees only a dream world of the future, unrelated to the present.[49]

When dealing with my health concerns, I was mentally farsighted in a way that made matters worse. I was focused on a future that statistically was not likely to happen. Making matters worse, this "future" was not a good one, and, once again, as Maxwell said, I was paying interest on a debt I may never owe—bad, bad, and bad.

Finally Maxwell has the following quote that he attributed to artist Andy Warhol: "They always say that time changes things, but you actually have to change them yourself."[50] This caused Maxwell to observe, "The truth is that any change that occurs in the world always begins first with change within an individual."[51]

Neither Warhol nor Maxwell qualified which change they were referring to, but I believe it is true for any change—personal or business.

You may have similar and even more dramatic stories to tell about the challenges in your life and are wondering where to start. Begin by believing that you understand what needs to be done (or soon will). Don't worry to what degree that is now true. At this moment, it matters only that you begin to think and act as though it is true. If you do, I can almost assure you that everything else will begin to fall into place.

Final Thoughts

In her 2008 article "The Universal Cycles of Change: Patterns in Nature Translated to Human Behavior," Kris Hallbom cited a conversation between Barbara Walters and Microsoft's Bill Gates in which Barbara asked Bill, "Now that you are the richest man in the world and you can have anything you desire, what more could you possibly want?"

Gates replied, "To never stop changing. Whatever I do today will be considered history tomorrow. I have to make sure that I never stop creating, and that I am always changing."[52]

I don't know Gates personally and cannot say with any certainty what he had in mind when he made those remarks. However, I can guess. He isn't talking about accumulating greater wealth just for the sake of having more money. Although he refers to his place in history, I seriously doubt that he is consumed by that, believing he must continue to achieve so as not to be forgotten.

Instead, I believe he is neatly summarizing the human condition. When we stop evolving, changing if you will, we are through, with the ultimate "stop" being death. When he says he has to "make sure that I never stop creating, and that I am always changing," I believe he recognizes the importance of continual, positive personal evolution.

We all change, even if we don't want to. The only uncertainty is whether personal change will happen at our direction or the direction of others. The answer to that depends on which of two choices we make:

- We can do little or nothing, allowing events to unfold as they will.
- We can proactively attempt to do what we can to bring about the change we wish to see.

Not surprisingly, I suggest you opt for the latter.

Researching and writing a book about the process of change has made me reflect on my own life, including all of the "certainties" that turned out to be not so certain after all.

Take a look at a list I might have created as I was beginning my career so long ago. If you are a member of my generation, much of this will sound familiar (and possibly amusing) to you. If you're younger (congratulations and condolences in equal measure), very little of this will resonate with you. However, rest assured that you will undoubtedly have your own list in thirty or forty years, one I wager will appear as naive and strange to you then as mine does to me now.

It's 1973, and this is what I know to be absolutely certain:

- Spending an entire career at one company is both possible and desirable.
- "Making your age" is the right yardstick for salaries.
- Employers frown on job-hopping. I will work for no more than three companies in my entire career.
- California real estate values will always rise, and, as a result, home equity will always be a solid retirement backstop, even if there is nothing else.
- Retirement accounts will always be there, as will Social Security. My retirement future is largely secured.
- The average cost of a new vehicle will continue to be approximately $4,000.
- Society will continue to stigmatize unmarried couples living together.
- Failed, isolated countries, particularly those with communist governments, such as Vietnam, North Korea, and the People's Republic of China, will remain unchanged, nonfactors in the world economy.
- The Beatles *will* reunite.

Clearly my certainties changed. Very little of what changed was under my control, whereas much of it affected me indirectly if not directly. Sitting on the sidelines, letting the world proceed without me, was not an option. I would have been dragged along regardless.

Fortunately for me, I am naturally proactive about change. Long before I considered it as a book topic, I was often unknowingly doing what I could to direct changes in my life. And now I not only recognize the importance of having done so, continuing to do so for whatever time remains to me, but also hope you do as well.

I'd like to end with a quotation from Charles Darwin that summarizes perfectly why I believe this topic is of such great importance: "It is not the strongest of the species that survive, nor the most intelligent, but the one most responsive to change."[53]

I couldn't have said it better myself.

Your Keys to the Kingdom

There are countless books full of advice on every subject imaginable, now including this one. Did you ever wonder how many of those who wrote those books actually do what they tell others to do?

The 7 Keys to Change outlines what I see as the ideal approach to change, but that doesn't mean reading it will ensure compliance—not for anyone, including me. We are, after all, human. Although this may be what we should do, doing it is often a completely different matter. But my hope is that simply reading and thinking about change as outlined in Part I, followed by the seven keys in Part II, will be the impetus for real, positive change for you in your personal and professional lives.

In the discussion of the seventh key (the importance of attitude), I described my own encounter with what I thought might be serious disease. Up until that point, I had not considered the importance of attitude. I was chronicling the forces behind change unknowingly almost missing the one thing I now consider the most critical element of all I had to say. So important that left unaddressed, I might never have finished this book.

However, I did ultimately come to realize the role attitude plays in our efforts to direct change, and, more importantly, I acted on what I learned. And now an update to that story may help substantiate that even more.

DO AS I SAY AND NOW AS I'VE DONE

My potentially significant health problem was my doctor's suspicion that I had prostate cancer. Today, I type those words and recall the feelings of dread that spread through me as he laid out the reasons for his concern (an elevated PSA [prostate-specific antigen] count). Being the professional he is, he could not give me the absolute assurances I would have liked, so I was left to make of my situation what I would. And if you read the seventh key, you know that initially it was not good.

Three months after that fateful conversation with my doctor and following preliminary visits to a urologist, I underwent a prostate biopsy with the results indicating "cell irregularity"—abnormal but not cancer, at least none detected by the biopsy.

This meant more testing, including another biopsy about nine months later, almost a year to the day after the initial concerns raised by the PSA test. This time there was no doubt regarding the findings; I had prostate cancer.

Just short of two months after the second biopsy, I underwent robotic prostatectomy to remove my prostate. There was a host of postsurgery "challenges" that I will spare you here, but suffice it to say, for a while, life was not as I knew it prior to the surgery. However, I got through that and have been declared cancer free by my doctor.

THE DIFFERENCE

Given a diagnosis of cancer followed by surgery and postsurgery recovery, you might assume I would have once again shut down as I briefly did based on just the suggestion of cancer. After all, if the mere possibility were sufficient to cause me to limit functioning, what would actually having the disease do?

But that was not the case.

The difference was, as Maxwell advised in *The Difference Maker: Making Your Attitude Your Greatest Asset*, I had learned the importance of understanding and controlling my attitude: "Your attitude really only becomes the difference maker when difficult challenges rise before you. In those moments, your attitude is sometimes the only difference between whether you press on or quit."[54] I pressed on, and you can too.

There is no diminishing the impact of this episode on my life, and it serves as a first-person account of the importance of the seventh key— one I hope you will consider carefully. However, there is one more, less dramatic postscript update I want to pass long as well.

THE SEVEN KEYS STRIKES A CHORD

The discussion of the third key ("The First Change Is in Your Mind—You Have to Want It") included my description of a lifelong, unfulfilled desire to learn to play guitar, accompanied by an also lifelong lack of a plan to make that happen. However, there is (relative) good news there, too.

A few months after writing the text for the third key, I once again decided to learn to play, this time preceded by creating a plan I hoped would bring better results. Unlike the past, I would now seek instruction and advice, and, of greatest importance, I committed to myself that practice would be an important element of the effort, both in duration and frequency.

My source for help has been the Internet, which by the way offers more free guitar-playing (and other instruments as well) instruction than you can possibly imagine or use. That, along with setting up a practice schedule I more or less adhere to, I am happy to say it's happening. I have learned more and can play better than at any time previously, and it all comes from following the advice detailed in *The 7 Keys of Change*.

These are just two of the countless changes that have occurred in my life since beginning this book. Although both are important to me, there is something more to be learned from this.

HOW YOU CHANGE, NOT IF

With or without the seven keys, one way or another I would have made it through my health challenge. The important question is, at what cost to my life in general? What else have I accomplished while dealing with prostate cancer that I might not have done had I not approached that unexpected, unwanted change as I ultimately did?

Looking back, we can probably rule out completing this book. If I had done no better with the confirmation of cancer than I did with the suggestion of its existence, my writing would have not only ground to a halt but also should have given the book's topic. But I ultimately did discover the importance of attitude when attempting to direct change, and hopefully you now have as well.

Now if I can just master the F major guitar chord.

NOTES

1. William Matthies, "Coyote Insight Change Survey" (unpublished data, 2010–2011).

2. Confucius," accessed September 13, 2012, http://www.quotationspage.com/quote/29767.html.

3. "The Costs of Failure: Economic Consequences of Failure to Enact Nixon, Carter, and Clinton Health Reforms," last modified March 26, 2010, accessed September 5, 2012, http://www.commonwealthfund.org/Content/Blog/The-Costs-of-Failure.aspx.

4. "Frequently Asked Questions," accessed September 5, 2012, http://www.sba.gov/sites/default/files/sbfaq.pdf.

5. "Helping Employees Embrace Change," last modified November 2002, accessed September 5, 2012, http://www.mckinseyquarterly.com/Helping_employees_embrace_change_1225.

6. "Making Change Work," accessed September 5, 2012, http://www-935.ibm.com/services/us/gbs/bus/html/gbs-making-change-work.html.

7. "Divorce Rate," accessed September 5, 2012, http://www.divorcerate.org.

8. "Fast Facts: Dropout Rates," accessed September 5, 2012, http://nces.ed.gov/fastfacts/display.asp?id=16.

9. "World Birth Rate," accessed September 5, 2012, http://www. indexmundi.com/world/birth_rate.html; "World Death Rate," accessed September 5, 2012, http://www.indexmundi.com/world/ death_rate.html.

10. "Bureau of Labor Statistics," accessed September 5, 2012, http://www.bls.gov/home.htm.

11. "Bureau of Labor Statistics," accessed September 5, 2012, http://www.bls.gov/home.htm.

12. "Bureau of Labor Statistics," accessed September 5, 2012, http://www.bls.gov/home.htm.

13. "Bureau of Labor Statistics," accessed September 5, 2012, http://www.bls.gov/home.htm.

14. "Bureau of Labor Statistics," accessed September 5, 2012, http://www.bls.gov/home.htm.

15. "Americans Getting Taller, Bigger, Fatter, Says CDC," accessed September 5, 2012, http://usgovinfo.about.com/od/healthcare/a/ tallbutfat.htm.

16. "Census of Housing," accessed September 5, 2012, http://www. census.gov/hhes/www/housing/census/historic/values.html; "Real Estate," accessed September 5, 2012, http://investmenttools.com/ median_and_average_sales_prices_of_houses_sold_in_the_ us.htm - median_and_average.

17. "Household Debt Service and Financial Obligations Ratios," last modified June 22, 2012, accessed September 5, 2012, http://www. federalreserve.gov/releases/housedebt.

18. Alan Murray, "The End of Management," Wall Street Journal, August 20, 2010, http://online.wsj.com/article/SB10001424052748 70447610457543972369557964.html.

19. Michael Scott, The Office, accessed September 13, 2012, http:// www.theofficequotes.com/season-6/sabre.

20. Silvia LaFair, *Don't Bring It to Work: Breaking the Family Patterns That Limit Success* (San Francisco: Jossey-Bass, 2009), Kindle ebook edition, location 440 of 4297.

21. Alan Murray, "The End of Management," Wall Street Journal, August 20, 2010, http://online.wsj.com/article/SB10001424052748 70447610457543972369557 9664.html.

22. Philip Kotler, *Marketing Management* (Englewood Cliffs, NJ: Prentice-Hall, Inc., 1967), page 149.

23. Joni E. Johnston, "How to Talk to a Depressed Employee," Psychology Today, June 10, 2010, http://www.psychologytoday.com/blog/the-human-equation/201006/how-talk-depressed-employee.

24. Timothy R. Clark, *EPIC Change: How to Lead Change in the Global Age* (New York: John Wiley & Sons, Inc., 2008), page 25.

25. "James Baldwin Quotes," accessed September 13, 2012, http://www.quotesnsayings.net/quotes/50583.

26. Silvia LaFair, *Don't Bring It to Work*, Kindle ebook edition, location 3480 of 4297.

27. Wayne W. Dyer, *Excuses Begone!: How to Change Lifelong, Self-Defeating Thinking Habits* (Carlsbad, CA: Hay House, Inc., 2009).

28. "Kurt Lewin," accessed September 5, 2012, http://en.wikipedia.org/wiki/Kurt_Lewin - Change_process.

29. "Kübler-Ross Model," accessed September 5, 2012, http://en.wikipedia.org/wiki/Kübler-Ross_model.

30. William Bridges, *Managing Transitions: Making the Most of Change* (Boston: DeCapo Press, 2009), page 100.

31. "Formula for Change," accessed September 5, 2012, http://en.wikipedia.org/wiki/Formula_for_Change.

32. "The Wealthy Mind™ Program," accessed September 5, 2012, http://thewealthymind.com/training/course-descripion.html.

33. John P. Kotter and Dan S. Cohen, *The Heart of Change* (Cambridge, MA: Harvard Business School Press, 2002).

34. Timothy R. Clark, *EPIC Change: How to Lead Change in the Global Age*.

35. "U.S. Vehicle Sales Market Share by Company, 1961–2011," accessed September 6, 2012, http://wardsauto.com/keydata/historical/UsaSa28summary/.

36. "Mistakes Made on the Road to Innovation," last modified November 26, 2006, accessed September 6, 2012, http://www.businessweek.com/stories/2006-11-26/mistakes-made-on-the-road-to-innovation.

37. "Kodak Reaffirms Plan to Complete Transformation to Sustainable, Profitable Company Starting 2012," last modified February 3, 2011, accessed September 6, 2012, Found at http://www.kodak.com/ek/ContentWithLeftCol.aspx?Pageid=28412&id=2147483761.

38. "Kodak Wins a Round in $1 Billion Apple, RIM Patent Dispute," last modified March 25, 2011, accessed September 6, 2012, http://www.bloomberg.com/news/2011-03-25/kodak-wins-round-in-1-billion-patent-case-against-apple-rim.html.

39. "Number, Timing, and Duration of Marriages and Divorces: 2001," last modified February 2005, accessed September 6, 2012, http://www.census.gov/prod/2005pubs/p70-97.pdf.

40. John C. Maxwell, *The Difference Maker: Making Your Attitude Your Greatest Asset* (Thomas Nelson Inc., 2006), Kindle ebook edition, location 31 of 1168.

41. John C. Maxwell, *The Difference Maker*, Kindle ebook edition, location 384 of 1168.

42. John C. Maxwell, *The Difference Maker*, Kindle ebook edition, location 385 of 1168.

43. John C. Maxwell, *The Difference Maker*, Kindle ebook edition, location 816 of 1168.

44. D. Martyn Lloyd-Jones, *Spiritual Depression: Its Causes and Cure* (Grand Rapids, MI: Eerdmans Publishing Company, 1965), page 20, cited in John C. Maxwell, *The Difference Maker*, Kindle ebook edition, location 466 of 1168.

45. John C. Maxwell, *The Difference Maker*, Kindle ebook edition, location 115 of 1168.

46. Napoleon Hill and W. Clement Stone, *Success Through a Positive Mental Attitude* (New York City, NY: Pocket Books, 1960, 1977).

47. Napoleon Hill and W. Clement Stone, *Success Through a Positive Mental Attitude*, Kindle ebook edition, location 30 of 342.

48. Wayne W. Dyer, *Excuses Begone!*, Kindle ebook edition, location 93 of 342.

49. Napoleon Hill and W. Clement Stone, *Success Through a Positive Mental Attitude*, Kindle ebook edition, location 113 of 342.

50. John C. Maxwell, *The Difference Maker*, Kindle ebook edition, location 590 of 1168.

51. John C. Maxwell, *The Difference Maker*, Kindle ebook edition, location 590 of 1168.

52. "The Wealthy Mind™ Program," accessed September 5, 2012, http://thewealthymind.com/training/course-descripion.html.

53. "Charles Darwin Quotes," accessed September 13, 2012, http://www.goodreads.com/author/quotes/12793.Charles_Darwin.

54. John C. Maxwell, *The Difference Maker*, Kindle ebook edition, location 384 of 1168.

INDEX

attitude
    change and, 72
    controlling, 133–138
    defined, 129–130
    importance of, 129
    role of, 143
automobile industry, 122

Beckhard, Richard, 101
Bridges, William, 101
business change. *See also* **personal change**
    batting average in, 2–3
    employee role in, 30, 67–70, 74, 97–98, 111
    examples of, 122–123
    failure to achieve, 12–13, 39, 67
    future of, 3–4
    goals in, 7–8, 86–87
    human element in, 39–40, 41, 43–45, 108
    inevitability of, 22–23
    management role in, 15–16, 40–45, 67–70, 74, 88
    market changes, 16–20
    myths of, 83–92
    negative effects on, 7–8
    obstacles to, 41
    personal change versus, x–xi, 7–8, 67, 100–101
    reacting to, 12–13, 23
    resistance to, 40
    semantics of, 73
    team for, 30–31, 73, 102, 113–114
    timing of, 121, 122–123
    track record in, 12–13

business planning. *See* plans/planning

change. *See also* business change; personal change
   attitudes toward, 1–7
   commitment to, 93–95, 145
   documenting, 105–108
   evolutionary versus revolutionary, 121–122, 127
   examples of, 14–15, 54–64, 78–80, 114–117
   excuses in, 96–97, 130
   forms of, 78, 101
   inevitability of, xi, 2, 4, 51
   information sources for, 5–6
   requirements for, 102, 103–105
   stages of, 101, 102–103
   templates for, 105–108
   timing of, 119–127
   traps in, 111–114, 117–118
   triggers for, 51–54, 65–66
   yardstick approach to, 24
change management. *See also* plans/planning
   effectiveness of, 28
   focus of, ix
   process of, 41–42
Clark, Timothy R., 70, 101, 102
Cohen, Dan S., 101, 102
consultants
   denial by, viii
   following advice of, viii–ix
   planning by, 28–29, 78, 137
consumer electronics industry
   change at Apple, 18–20
   early history of, 16–18, 21–22
   market evolution in, 22–23
   technology in, 20–23
costs
   of doing nothing, 11–12
   effect of, 31
   in failed marriages, 13–14
   goals versus tactics, 42–43, 104–105, 112–113
   hidden costs, 21
   personal versus personnel, 88

ABOUT THE AUTHOR

William Matthies

In 1986, William Matthies founded what was to become the largest independent market research and database marketing company in the consumer electronics and high-tech industries. By the time he sold it in 1997, The Verity Group employed more than four hundred people at its California and Costa Rica offices.

Prior to that, Bill cofounded Barcus Berry Electronics Inc., a venture capital-backed start-up with a proprietary audio technology called BBE, which was licensed for use in audio, video, computing, and telecommunication products.

From 1977 to 1983, he wore several hats at Pioneer Electronics (USA) Inc., including director of market research, director of sales planning, national sales manager special markets, vice president of marketing, and, ultimately, senior vice president of marketing and product development.

Today, Bill serves on corporate advisory boards, is a contributor to TWICE (the CE industry's major trade publication), and lectures frequently at industry events around the world on customer relations, strategic planning, and change management.

www.ingramcontent.com/pod-product-compliance
Lightning Source LLC
Chambersburg PA
CBHW060029210326
41520CB00009B/1053